The Astrological Dynamics of the Universe

1970-2020: the Crisis Point

The Astrological Dynamics of the Universe

1970-2020: the Crisis Point

Demian Allan

BOOKS

Winchester, UK
Washington, USA

First published by O-Books, 2012
O-Books is an imprint of John Hunt Publishing Ltd., Laurel House, Station Approach,
Alresford, Hants, SO24 9JH, UK
office1@jhpbooks.net
www.johnhuntpublishing.com

For distributor details and how to order please visit the 'Ordering' section on our website.

Text copyright: Demian Allan 2012

ISBN: 978 1 78099 439 0

A CIP catalogue record for this book is available from the British Library.

Design: Stuart Davies

Printed and bound by CPI Group (UK) Ltd, Croydon, CR0 4YY

We operate a distinctive and ethical publishing philosophy in all
areas of our business, from our global network of authors to
production and worldwide distribution.

CONTENTS

Acknowledgements

Thank you to my wife Amanda for her patience and understanding during the writing of this book and for her constant encouragement. I would also like to thank everyone at Watkins Books. Thanks also to Etan for his enthusiasm and for giving me the opportunity and deadlines that allowed me to complete the book.

Introduction

Through the planetary cycles that we are all about to experience, we will open up our world view to a more universal view, meaning our perception of planet Earth is about to change. I have been studying astrology for over twenty-five years and during that period have experienced the many facets of the planets' transits and progressions on an individual scale and through clients' experiences. Astrology works symbolically and systematically as a divination technique. The Moon's monthly cycle is one aspect of how our Solar System has a direct link with what happens down here on Earth, coining the expression 'as above, so below'. In the Moon's cycle, the New Moon (when the Sun and Moon are in the same constellation sign) heralds a chance to begin new projects and ventures, whereas after this event we have the waxing period of the Moon, which is a time when we move forward in life. This leads to the Full Moon cycle when the Sun and Moon are in opposition with each other causing endings and acute emotional anxieties but also a degree of creativity. Following on from the Full Moon we have the Waning Moon that symbolically takes away our natural energies encouraging us to slow down in life. This eventually culminates in the Dark Moon before we come full circle to the New Moon.

The orbit of the Moon is just one aspect of astrology that gives us an indicator of how a planet or star can directly link in with our everyday lives. Astrology is able to point us in the right direction as regards how we relate to the world, and the responses of other humans – emotionally, politically and of course spiritually. In this book I have tried to look at the cycles of the outer planets (Jupiter, Saturn, Uranus, Neptune and Pluto) over the last forty years (1970–2011) and the next eight years (2012–2020). This will enable us to see how past astrological cycles have affected us and will also give us an idea of what we can expect and how it will manifest over the next eight years and beyond. *The Astrological Dynamics of the Universe* is an introduction to these cycles and to each planet's vibration when travelling through a particular sign of the zodiac, including the implications of that combination. As a full-time working astrologer I am interested not only in the individual patterns of a natal chart but also the more mundane aspects of astrology, which is why I have included the natal charts of the United Kingdom and the United States of America. The aim of this book is for the reader to have a better understanding of how the astrological cycles work within the structure of the universal law. Everything that we send out to the universe has an energy, and that energy at some point directs back at us. Therefore we must respect it and work with it so that we may have a future on this beautiful planet Earth.

Chapter 1

The Plutonic Crisis

Much has been written about the year 2012 – it has almost mythical status in our collective unconsciousness. As the months have passed, bringing us closer and closer to this giant of a year, we humans have become anxious about the future and how it will develop. Astrology is a tool that can enable us as humans to investigate and predict the cycles that are upon us at a rapid rate. But before we can judge how we will respond to the energetic pull of the planets and their aspects, we first need to look at the historical and cultural implications of planetary movements.

In the build-up to 2012 we have already seen upheaval and strife; however, that is part of human evolution, emotionally, mentally and of course spiritually. Pluto is the planet of transformation and destruction; in its cycle through the constellations it can take up to twenty-four years to travel through one sign of the zodiac. Looking at Pluto's position and impact in the past and indeed over the last forty years can help us to find a connection with the future and its energetic shifts. Pluto in recent history has travelled in the signs of Libra, Scorpio and Sagittarius, and so we have seen in a short time a shift and a tearing down of old structures. Pluto stands for rebirth and is the ruler of the zodiac sign of Scorpio, dictating the underworld currents that dominate the subtlety of Pluto. It is a planet that on an individual level does not strive to jolt you into action like the planet Uranus, but allows a slow build-up of emotions and blockages that start to have an impact internally and then externally. Put it this way, a husband who has Pluto transiting the partnership sector of his chart might not want a divorce, but his wife (externally) could; therefore the reaction from the husband is a need to transform in order to survive. Pluto works in that way, you could say in mysterious undercurrents that can bring out those emotions we generally call negative, jealously being one. On a global level, Pluto rules the 'darker' aspects of our consciousness, the aspects that we would rather not see in the world. It brings with it upheavals, drastic changes in the human condition that can be for good or for evil depending on the sign it occupies at that moment in history.

In the year 1972 Pluto entered the sign of Libra, the zodiac sign of justice and partnerships ruled by Venus. Pluto stayed within Libra up until 1984, causing a shift in the way that relationships were conducted in the western world, meaning old structures were torn down. This not only included the adults that were under the direct rays of Pluto at the time of this transit, but also the children who were born at this time. The semiotic shift of the sixties generation made the boundaries of family life and particular relationships blurred, as these baby boomers were born with the rebellious planet Uranus in Cancer, seeking to destroy the family set-up. As Pluto started to enter the sign of Libra, the focus on relationships and gender started to become much more apparent. The direct result of this manifestation is the breakdown of partnerships, or at least that people were trying to find a balance in a world when more options were becoming more available, for example sexual experimentation, the Feminist Movement and gender questioning all become healthy outlets that needed to be explored. However, Pluto always seeks to destroy old patterns of behaviour. When boundaries become uncertain, humans begin to feel lost in a maze of confusion, unsure of the correct emotional responses, and the effects are still being felt in the twenty-first century. During Pluto's cycle through Libra (1972–1984) we saw an increase in divorce rates. It also gave rise to different permutations of the family unit, including commune living and the swapping of gender roles, the 'house husband' role becoming more prominent while women were becoming more involved and independent in the workforce. This typifies the Libran need for equality and balance; however, it is an adjustment that can take time to settle, therefore creating new boundaries. Most of these ideas were ideals (Venus) rather than explosive reactions to the status quo; the hippy dream for many, coupled with the need for consumerism, created juxtapositions in modes of mood and behaviour. It is only when Pluto enters its own sign of Scorpio that we really start to feel the Plutonic shift. It is as if our last waltz in the Piscean age is conducted before we enter the great Aquarian age. Death and regeneration become key symbols for this period in the past. We see a rise in conflict as well as cultural transformation that leads to political upheaval and a revolution in artistic expression; think about the alternative comedy scene that gave rise to a rather caustic and political edge to our sense of humour: Ben Elton, Spitting Image, Bill Hicks. However, some revealing and positive messages were bought to our consciousness. Death became the 'anchor' of the Live Aid concert in 1985, as the Ethiopian people experienced famine. In other words, a cry was heard to break the structures (Pluto) and transform (Scorpio) charitable events. Bob Geldof (a Libra with Sagittarius rising) tapped into the energy of Pluto to create something powerful through the medium of music (Libran) which would raise the plight of the Ethiopians (Pluto). The stark images that were played out to millions of individuals on that day not only brought about a higher consciousness in our thinking, but also brought about the abstract thought of the world becoming smaller. Pluto has that shift, it can destroy as well as transform, and it is not wholly negative in action. The rise at this time in government institutions and capitalism is another shift in Pluto's action in the period 1984–1995. Remember that Scorpio is a fixed sign; it can therefore be unrelenting in its ambition. Our future and culture started to be moulded at this point in time – from music, films and of course television, a slow-burning revolution indeed. One of the other major aspects with Pluto and Scorpio is the rise in sexual diseases, in particular Aids. No other combination (Pluto travelling in Scorpio) could be as potent in terms of sexual issues. Oil (underground, the Hades myth) becomes a feature with the Gulf War in the early nineties. During this period a rapid rise in the capitalist market paved the way for the next shift, as Pluto entered Sagittarius.

Moving on from the energy of Scorpio which drives the underworld, we now come to the philosophical musings of the archer. The sign of Sagittarian energy is one of boundless optimism, ruled by expansive Jupiter; it also comes under the rulership of education, spirituality, travel, different cultures, religion and greed. In 1995, Pluto began its journey through the sign of Sagittarius, finishing in 2008. This is a period when the world became smaller and when it was easier to travel; the Eurostar is an excellent example of Pluto (underground) coming together with Sagittarius (travel). Two world leaders who embodied the Sagittarian framework of optimism and religious connotations were Bill Clinton (Leo) and Tony Blair (Taurus). The semiotic shift in temperament from the greed of Scorpio to the buoyancy of Sagittarius was directly expressed by the actions of these two politicians. Although Clinton became President in 1992, his organisation skills and ability to communicate effectively conjoined with the Jupiter rays of the time. However, with expansion comes complacency, as we humans gather and gather more and therefore expect instant gratification (Jupiter). Our mindsets change, and globalisation is the negative effect of Pluto's passage through Sagittarius. Religion and its doctrines start to become the focal point in decisions, for example Tony Blair felt through his religious beliefs a justification for invading Iraq, as well as a focus on Islamic extremism. This is again a negative aspect of Pluto through Sagittarius, for the archer can become dogmatic through their beliefs and principles. Another aspect at this time was the rise in 'new age' comments and views. This rise served to break down the boundaries of religion and our connection with a God.

The passage of Pluto through these three signs (Libra, Scorpio and Sagittarius) gave rise to great political and cultural shifts, which have moulded and shaped our immediate future. We move from the air sign of Libra, signalling communication, partnerships and idealism, to the fixed water sign of Scorpio, creating storms and unseen realties, to the fire of Sagittarius, bringing a sense of adventure and moving forward. The bridge that is created during this period is one of expectation and changing moral standards that try to keep up with the technology as we enter the Aquarian age. Pluto acts as a vehicle, forcing us to go through a metamorphosis that can bring in destruction and clear the debris for a new dawn. How we respond to Pluto's energy, remembering that it is energy that slowly builds up, will indicate what will be transformed.

In the year 2008, Pluto entered the zodiac sign of Capricorn, and it is with this shift that we truly come to a Plutonic crisis point. Capricorn is an earth sign, signalling the materialistic quality of the sign. It also rules by the planet of limitations, Saturn, the great wise old teacher, cultivating strict measures from our expansive Sagittarian energy that we have enjoyed and abused. Jupiter and Saturn work very much together, as Jupiter gives with limitless gestures, while Saturn demands attention to detail. This should create a nice balance; however, if one has been abused (in this case Jupiter) then the other comes down harder. So, Saturn is going to come down heavy on us all. Pluto wants to shake the foundations and Saturn wants to make sure the foundations are solid, thus you have a conflict. When Pluto entered the sign of Capricorn in 2008, just two weeks later the first signs of the financial meltdown began to be exposed. This is how Pluto can break structures, through governmental institutions and financial outlets. So we come back to the last thirty years, and how what we have shaped is now going to be broken down and restructured. Capricorn rules the work sector of our lives, our ambition and our need to gather status among our peers. But this action can lead us to be guilty of creating a culture that is built upon what you have, what you need, and which misses the more spiritual side of our lives. Capricorn being an earth sign, it will also bring in and destroy the agriculture industry in the world. This has already begun, in particular in the United Kingdom, and I will look at this in more detail later on. Pluto also will find a way to bring in more natural disasters; the earth (Capricorn) will literally shake (Pluto). It is as if Hades wants to come back from the underworld and create destruction through his wrath. Through the period of 2012 to 2024 Pluto will be travelling through Capricorn – the question is: what will be the extent of its destruction and rebirth?

Pluto wants to come to this crisis point; we are missing vital aspects of our own spiritual development (I will come to Neptune later) and Pluto if anything is not superficial. Pluto wants to work with the universal law that everything that we as humanity send out (every energetic thought and action), the universe will send back, positive or negative. However, the restrictions that have been put into place by governments and corporations are more about mass control and manipulation; they have created the new boundaries that must be torn down. Pluto is not bound by human laws, or indeed intellectual arguments. What is important is that the 'survival' factor of we humans becomes our mantra as a collective, not as individuals, and therein lies the difference. Pluto is forcing us to this crisis point so that we get a second chance to create and respect our place on this planet Earth.

Chapter 2

This State of Emergency

One planet that can have a profound effect on the cosmic force of us humans is the planet Uranus. This planet is the ruler of the zodiac sign of Aquarius and its energy is revolutionary in attitude as well as in action. Uranus wants to tear down the structures in a more impulsive way than Pluto, for Pluto is the destroyer and Uranus is the awakener. From time to time, humanity needs to use the higher octave vibrations of Uranus that in terms of activity work on a higher vibration than those of the planet Mercury. Through the actions of questioning and rebelling we are able to gather and reap the rewards of lost and future knowledge. Uranus conveys this quality, the energy, like in the myth of Prometheus who stole fire from the gods to help humanity – but with rebellion comes punishment. Uranus means historically that all those individuals born with strong aspects to Uranus in their natal chart have had to be slightly left-field in their attitudes and opinions, sometimes leaving them open to ridicule. This energetic process is the reason why Uranus is the planet most associated with the term 'genius'. For Uranus is that flash of inspiration, that eureka moment that seems to just pop into the mind, forging new insights in science, technology, psychology and spirituality.

In determining both how our consciousness as humans has been developed through Uranus' energy, and to what extent we can expect Uranus to save us or break us, I shall look at the last forty years of Uranus' journey through the zodiac signs. Within these years Uranus has travelled through the signs Virgo, Libra, Scorpio, Sagittarius, Capricorn, Aquarius, Pisces and of course

Aries. Uranus works on a seven-year cycle of staying in each sign for near enough that period of time, depending on its orbit. The proof that Uranus is travelling through a sign at a particular time will be where humanity needs to awaken and adjust to the tremors of rebellion and higher insight. For example in the early seventies Uranus travelled through Virgo transferring to Libra. This gave rise to health matters and the alternative culture of the late sixties through meditation, mind-expanding (Mercury) drugs and political upheavals. By the time that Uranus moved into Libra the focus was on personal relationships (coupled of course with Pluto in Libra) and we saw the biggest shift in the justice system in relation to the institution of marriage. Uranus wants to break free and do what it wants to do and with whom! This potent energy gave rise to instability in relationships and provided new insights into sexual experimentation. Uranus is an asexual planet that wishes to break the boundaries in that arena. This was mainly manifested through artistic expression (Libra/Venus) in musical icons like David Bowie (Capricorn), Marc Bolan (Libra) and the Glam Movement in the early mid-seventies. Homosexuality, bisexuality, partner-swapping and general 'gender bending' became a focal point under the guidance of Uranus. Of course this was not happening in every street in the UK or US. However, figureheads like Bowie were drawing down Uranus' energy (lost knowledge) and becoming the water bearers (in their archetypal role) to help us become more conscious of these taboos. Remember that Libra is a cardinal sign – this quality wants to forge ahead and break new ground, and it has ambition. One major act of Uranus in Libra was the emergence of the Freedom of Information Act in the United States after the Watergate scandal. This is where Uranus energy can help humanity become more equal across the spectrum. If we look to people in history who have made a profound mark on the world a strong Aquarian/Uranian theme runs through their charts. Note the following personalities with the Sun in Aquarius: Charles Dickens, Thomas Edison, Charles Darwin, Lewis Carroll, Abraham Lincoln, Francis Bacon, James Dean, Bob Marley, Virginia Woolf and Germaine Greer. Also Karl Marx, a Taurus with a strong Uranus on his MC. Even Aquarius rising: Jim Morrison, Janis Joplin, Renoir, Degas, Robert Louis Stevenson and glam rocker David Bowie. All have made very individual offerings to the world and have shown an uncanny ability to tap into a world closely associated with Uranus' inspiration.

In 1975 Uranus moved into the secretive and explosive sign of Scorpio, bringing disharmony and violent change. This combination of anger and dissatisfaction with the status quo was reflected in the musical Punk Movement spearheaded funnily enough by three Aquarians from different ends of the spectrum: John Lydon, Malcolm McLaren and the fashion designer Vivienne Westwood. But as new movements were beginning, ie the rise of television, home gadgets, computers and film, endings also became apparent. At this time the hippy dream had died for many people. Scorpio wants to dig deep and Uranus is not content with what it has. This is what I would best describe as a first crisis point, when the old and the new begin to feel the strain. Many people were killed in the earthquake in China in 1976 as Pluto in Libra combined with the Uranus/Scorpio shift. Margaret Thatcher earned the nickname the 'Iron Lady'; a Libra (Pluto) with Scorpio rising, it is no wonder she moved into power in 1979 for she embodied the 'want' of the United Kingdom for change and drastic action. At this time Pluto was crossing the UK's natal chart of Libra rising. Scorpio and Uranus have their conflicts because the basic function of Scorpio is to hold close, while Uranus wants to break free. This dichotomy only eased in 1982 when Uranus entered and settled in the zodiac sign of Sagittarius. Uranus is more comfortable in Jupiter, as the need for space and freedom is given acceptance by the archer. However Uranus is not going to stand still and stop rebelling; in fact you could say that it is speeded up now that it is engaged with the mutable energy of Sagittarius. The travel industry accelerated as well and there were new educational (Sagittarius) insights (Uranus). One of the major factors of Uranus entering Sagittarius is that the work ethic changed; it was a time for the self-starters in business to reach for their ambitions. We see a 'risk'-taking culture that uses the freewheeling Jupiter energy and looks at the big picture. Uranus and Jupiter work well together – we have the flash of inspiration from Uranus and the scope of Jupiter's thinking, helping us to make big plans. However, during this transit we can be led away from looking at the details, and therefore we can literally over-expand ourselves. What we experienced during this period is an opportunist (Jupiter) and eccentric (Uranus) nature that led to a focus in the UK as well as the US on increasing work hours and technology (Uranus), in particular replacing jobs within factories. The pace of technology should not be underestimated, since this period brought about one of the biggest shake-ups, notably computers becoming a common feature in the workplace.

It is only in 1988 that we had another shift and perhaps an indicator of the activity over the next ten years when Uranus along with Saturn moved into the austere zodiac sign of Capricorn. Remember that Uranus is the ruler of Aquarius and Saturn is the ruler of Capricorn; however, the sign of Aquarius used to be ruled by Saturn. The energy of the 'crazy' world of Uranus does not sit well with the restrictive and materialistic view of Capricorn. Therefore the focus is on financial (Capricorn) matters and reversals of fortune. These are the first signs that another recession is about to hit the western world, for Uranus finds it hard to curb its attitude and so brings about unexpected instability to governmental institutions. The tearing down of the Berlin Wall is a good example of Uranus' rays bringing disruption to tradition (Capricorn). That's how Uranus works – it clears the clutter from the past to bring in a new dawn. However, during this seven-year period from 1988 onwards we see that Uranus is not comfortable in its habitation, for Capricorn will always try to resist the temptation to stray and break the bonds from the past. Although, not only did we see the end of the Cold War but also the end of apartheid in South Africa, events that managed to go above the Capricorn status and take inspiration from the humanitarian instincts of Uranus. During this period the UK's Prime Minister John Major (an Aries but with Capricorn rising) took over office, bringing us the statement 'back to basics'. But you cannot hide from Uranus; like a bolt of lightning it will come and reawaken new values. In Greek mythology Uranus was the father of the sky and of Cronus and Rhea. His power is direct and destructive, as regards what he sees as needing to be changed. Any alternative movements will be initiated by Uranus, and all revolutions come under this banner. However, like most revolutions the Uranus uprising is not a peaceful protest (that is more in keeping with Neptune). It is a need to tear down what is no longer seen as necessary, and it is a desire to bring in changes that will help humanity become more equal. You could say that there is a certain amount of idealism here, and this is true. However, once the old has been destroyed you need the structure of, say, Saturn to maintain what has been changed. This is where Uranus can have problems. It's great to be able to change things, but a plan needs to develop and you need to allow time for it to grow into something that will have a lasting effect for the good. This is how the zodiac signs Capricorn and the planet Saturn can really function at their best. Structures need to be implemented in order to gain development. During the period 1988 to 1995 we find that there was a certain push and pull dalliance that kept the world in a state of perpetual limbo. Culturally we saw a shift in perception, as the Grunge (musical) Movement from the States totally encapsulated the austerity of

Capricorn through the image of the rebellion and sound of Uranus (electricity is ruled by Uranus). We also saw that Capricorn's influence took its form in clothes and aesthetics, as we used plain colours to express ourselves – grey, beige and white being prominent in expression.

In 1995, we saw Uranus move into its own sign of Aquarius. Uranus is now allowed to express itself freely and without restriction. The fixed determination of the Aquarian energy comes as a stable outlet for the genius of Uranus. An embodiment of this combination is how the internet gained a higher profile and revolutionised the way we communicate and gain information. The internet (born at a time when Aquarius was rising) uses the Uranus principles of freedom of expression, lost knowledge and technology through the cosmos. This gives the layperson the power of speech and enables people who are on the fringes of society to communicate with like-minded individuals. But as most of us who have some knowledge of astrology will know, Aquarians can be unpredictable and sometimes a little perverse in their actions. The arts became active again in the popular consciousness. Artists like Damien Hirst (Gemini) and Tracey Emin (Cancer) use shocking but inventive avenues for their artistic creations. The musical forms in the UK tend to take on the mantle of the late sixties with bands like Blur, Oasis and Pulp mirroring the Beatles, Stones and The Kinks. Of course in 1997 we had a big shift in the political arena as the Labour Government came in to power. Tony Blair (Aquarius Moon) advanced his cause by using the media and technology to gain access and spread his message; again think of the symbol of the water bearer. But just as Uranus became comfortable in Aquarius in 2002 it moved into the nebulous sign of Pisces, the zodiac sign of endings and dreams. The erratic energy of Uranus is suddenly turned upside-down as it enters the depths of Pisces, with its illusions and creative flair. Uranus is likely to sink in the water signs and bring chaos to their waters. Think of Uranus in Cancer in the early fifties and how the generation born at that time became dissatisfied with the restrictions of the family unit. Or those born with Uranus in Scorpio who are now keener to explore their own inner depths through sexual and technological escapes, internet pornography being one vehicle. Uranus does not have clarity within the water signs, although Pisces is perhaps one of the easiest because of its mutable quality. However, it has seen a period of confusion, the Iraq War which led many to believe that we were fed wrong information from the Government – this is a typical Uranus in Pisces combination. Secrets are not so secret when Pisces and Uranus collide. However, Uranus is going to be given a new lease of life as it now enters the cardinal sign of Aries, signalling a new eighty-four-year cycle. We are about to embark on this state of emergency.

Chapter 3

Take a Ride on My Magic Carpet

If Pluto is the destroyer and Uranus is the awakener, then Neptune is the visionary. But sometimes, just sometimes, visions can get distorted. Neptune is a catalyst for our unconscious; it is nebulous in its inner workings and is not tangible in form. What Neptune wants us humans to do is to have faith and sacrifice our ego for the greater good. Venus wants to love one person, Neptune wants to love several, and therefore Neptune individuals (those with Pisces or Neptune on the angles) tend to suffer from naïvety and other people's unhealthy projections. The thing about Neptune is that it's subtle; it is not as strong as Pluto or as obvious as Uranus, it hovers under the surface, then suddenly a volcano of emotion erupts. Over the last forty years Neptune has gone through four signs of the zodiac: Sagittarius, Capricorn, Aquarius and Pisces. The time it takes Neptune to travel through one sign is about fourteen years, again depending on its orbit. We start off in the year 1970 as Neptune entered the sign of Sagittarius. One of the significant focal points with this combination is that in relation to religion and the occult. Interest in eastern religion and philosophy started to occur in the sixties within a select group; however, by the early seventies the mystical had begun to appear in the more mainstream sectors. Neptune in Sagittarius is keenly aware of the importance of faith and a trust in the universal and occult laws. Astrology itself becomes more widely available as do tarot, numerology, runes and alternative therapies. This includes the introduction of these subjects to the educational establishment, with courses in adult colleges in the UK and the US. It is perhaps the disintegration of Christianity that helped to fuel the fire of self-exploration. In

March 1848 the start of spiritualism in the West was a direct influence of the need to delve into the hidden realms – Neptune in one degree in Pisces. Pisces being as mutable as Sagittarius, wants to be more fluid in action, and spiritualism is a set of principles that bases itself on more direct experiences with the 'other side'. In the 1970's we saw this attitude resonate again in our collective unconsciousness as we sought to understand (naïvely) higher dimensions. This gave rise to the 'guru' who would attract disciples who would then become disillusioned (Neptune) by their prophet (Sagittarius). One example of this is the mystic Osho (Sagittarius), who was at the height of his charismatic power in terms of followers and ashrams, and was dedicated to his teachings throughout Neptune's journey in Sagittarius. The crossing of boundaries is always an issue when this planet is involved, because Neptune hates to feel any kind of restriction, but not in the same way as Uranus. Neptune wants the boundaries to be fuzzy and diluted. However, with insight can come illusion, and this is Neptune's big downfall, because the basic desire of Neptune is to escape. We find that drugs (Neptune) in all forms (legal or non-legal) became more actively used at this junction in time. The need to transcend and become one with the universe becomes a more potent force as there is the need to escape from the earthly planes. However, the need and impulse to do this is in keeping with the Sagittarian energy of the explorer through the mind, body and spirit. Drugs from 'other' cultures start to appeal on a wider scale, and we notice a thirst to broaden our cultural horizons in the West.

Neptune is not there to deceive (although in most cases it does) but to allow humans to reach and experience a higher state of consciousness, even if it is just for a fleeting moment. Within that sphere, a new way of looking at the cycle of life and its nuances is experienced and understood. Therefore the arts and creative expression come under Neptune's rays. This is because the 'artist' becomes the object that is channelled full of inspiration from a higher source. Neptune looks for the non-tangible in life and seeks to unite us with the God form. But first Neptune teaches us that we must sacrifice before we can enter the positive void of its realms. Anybody who is under Neptune's rays will either be an inspired individual or a complete wreck unable to deal with the reality of day-to-day living. If we look at historical figures who have this planet dominating their natal chart we can begin to see a pattern. Marilyn Monroe (Neptune ASC), Aleister Crowley (Neptune MC), Prince (Neptune MC), Bob Dylan (Neptune ninth house), Jimi Hendrix (Neptune ninth house), Elizabeth Taylor (Pisces), Albert Einstein (Pisces), Kurt Cobain (Pisces) and Princess Diana (Neptune ASC). One aspect unites these individuals and this is creative inspiration. However, another aspect that is a defining feature of Neptune is controversy. Neptune's rays become a filter for other people's dreams and therefore expectations can become too great and eventually come crashing down. Then we seek a kind of redemption through sacrifice, again that word sacrifice always comes into the view of Neptune. The film industry also comes under the rulership of Neptune and it is during Neptune's passage through Sagittarius that we see an increase in the output of films and experimentation. For instance, the utopian dream of the goodies against the baddies in *Star Wars*, the fear-infested waters of *Jaws*, and the inducement of horror in *The Exorcist*. The camera creates through its own projection a world that is like the one we know but also different. The camera transports us to other dimensions but can give a distorted view. We as the audience or viewer, however, interrupt the images based on our own experiences. Neptune becomes the lens; it distorts and deceives the viewer.

In 1984 we saw another shift in energy, as Neptune began its journey through the zodiac sign of Capricorn. Gone is the philosophical and over-indulgent nature of Sagittarius, and in steps the materialistic and ambitious Capricorn, so we now have the illusionary with the realistic. This combination can actually work very well, as long as the boundaries are made clear. During this period we saw the rise in globalisation and corporate companies deceiving (Neptune) the masses – think of the medical companies. The shift in spirituality became more money-orientated than ever, as a shift in consumerism and 'easy access' spirituality started to become an entire industry. The effect of Neptune on Capricorn is to sell the abstract, the nebulous, as an attractive package. The Capricorn wants to dominate and make sense of the Neptune energy, because on a fundamental level it does not understand it at first. While the Sagittarius was happy to play with Neptune, Capricorn wants to use Neptune for gain. The glamour (Neptune) of success and worldly ambitions reach fever pitch at these times and films like *Wall Street* become the new archetypes for a generation. However, with greed and power come responsibility and uncharted boundaries which mean new financial problems for the world. The 1980's saw a mass wave in entrepreneurs creating new rules in terms of work and employment that were different from their parents' generation. We saw the glitz of the business world take shape with champagne lifestyles and unbounded dreams being fulfilled materialistically. This is when Neptune can literally take us up the garden path; all looks well for a while and then the dream begins to fade. By the start of the nineties the dream for many was beginning to fall away. Remember that Capricorn is ruled by the planet Saturn that likes to impose restrictions on us. So as we get carried away with Neptune's glamour financially, Saturn takes away the shine. But as I said, Neptune is always chameleon-like in its actions and therefore it finds a way of creating a false reality through another medium. That medium becomes the start of celebrity culture in the West, when the first murmurs of exposing the illusion (Neptune) of the money-making (Capricorn) celebrity. One Capricorn who rose to success during this period is the British model Kate Moss (Capricorn) who becomes the embodiment of what is termed 'cool' within the industry. Kurt Cobain (Pisces/Uranus) also delivers and projects for a generation the false hope and empathy of a youth culture that struggles to comprehend the future according to its world view. Governments start to give mixed messages that are becoming more obvious in their intentions. By the close of the millennium Neptune has exhausted itself in Capricorn and begins to enter the humanitarian sign of Aquarius, gathering pace for the Aquarian age. Much has been made of this 'new dawn' when Aquarian principles will become the very beacon of our society. But what must be remembered is that Aquarius is an air sign while Neptune is the depths of the great ocean; on basic terms they cook up a storm. The desire for advancement and dreams of the mystical Neptune coupled with the utopian-minded Aquarius allow the illusionary world to really begin to take off. It's easy to allow the optimism and Aquarian principles to override the need for balance and an objective view. Neptune's passage through Aquarius has seen and created a society that is based on the individual rather than the community. This is the more negative essence of Aquarius' energy; it prefers a voyeuristic nature to getting more intimately involved. This can create a separation of the senses and the body, since Aquarius is an air (mind) sign and Neptune prefers dreams to reality. The combination exerts a rather idealistic view, and since 1998 society has begun to shape itself on dreams and forbidden fruit rather than the basic need for survival.

As we reach 2012, Neptune's clouds have made us unsure of where humanity is going. The combination of the outer planets of Pluto, Uranus and Neptune have shifted our planet Earth into new territories, and while Neptune has stirred up storms and environmental damages, the hope and faith in our future rests with us. Neptune wants the boundaries to be less clear in order to make way for more creative thinking. This is so that we can reach that higher state of consciousness.

Chapter 4

Jupiter Embraces Saturn

In dealing with world events and their causes and influences, we need to look at two planets that have a direct bearing on energies and connections with the universe. As humans we are on this small planet Earth trying to build and enjoy our life, but within the framework of the universe, we are a mere speck – a part of the bigger spectrum. We have all experienced moments when we have felt a heightened awareness of periods in time, a hint of a parallel life or a *déjà vu*. The trick for us all is to realise that we are all as one, connected to the universe, and that our experience has an effect on others around us, following the karmic laws of universal thinking. Unfortunately, as humans we become scared in our thought-life and then process this thinking, therefore becoming over-protective of our own needs. This leads to selfish actions and 'panic thinking', and this process stops us creating and being our true self. Easier said than done, in other words the point is that we do have a focal point. As nature teaches us on a regular basis, we all have a role that fits in with our environment, sometimes beautiful and sometimes brutal. The planets work in cycles and their rays influence and direct us from one energetic shift to another; it is up to us as humans how we respond and in turn bear the consequences.

The planets Jupiter and Saturn work closely with each other; they are brothers as well as enemies that have a great deal to learn from each other. When one dominates, the sky's balance is thrown out, causing strife and upheaval. Jupiter's message is simple: it wants expansion through the mind, the physical and the spiritual. The Greek god Zeus is the symbol for Jupiter, the great Father of the sky, who demands too much and is quite self-indulgent in his actions. There are times when as individuals we need to look at the broader view, see the big picture; this is when Jupiter is a benefit. Because the nature of Jupiter is benevolant, it brings a certain amount of luck or at least a trust in the cosmos. This is because Jupiter has faith in the future, therefore the planet has religious connotations attached to it. However, the reverse side of Jupiter's rays is that of too much faith and not enough planning – that's Saturn's job. Jupiter can achieve a great deal in a short space of time, in the active pursuit of its objectives. The sign that Jupiter rules is Sagittarius, it also used to be (before Neptune was discovered) the ruler of the zodiac sign Pisces. Both signs are mutable in nature; they change to the circumstance that is presented to them. However, it is true for both of these signs that they are better off starting projects and ideas than completing them – this is within the context of natal astrology. Jupiter also brings in an idealism in world affairs that is necessary as a concept, especially in political ideologies. Saturn is the great teacher in the sky; it is the planet of limitations and restrictions that can also bring in solid results to hard-earned efforts. If Jupiter is the optimistic university professor, then Saturn is the principal, educating through rules and regulations within a strict code of ethics. This is how the combination of these two planets works; they operate in tandem with each other, supporting and nurturing.

The historical significance of these two powerhouse planets demonstrates the shift of consciousness and the ultimate state of our future. When these two meet in the celestial skies even by conjunction, opposition, trine or square, a shift in our world view occurs depending on the signs that are involved. The conjunction of Jupiter and Saturn (which is a major aspect) occurs every twenty years. The last one happened in the year 2000, which was a rather appropriate kick-start for the new millennium. This conjunction can provide insight and also a sense of a new beginning. This, however, can lead to over-optimism that can create problems, times when we as humanity are left picking up the pieces. These two planets can work for and against each other depending on the influences of the other outer planets. So if we look into history we see an opposition between these two planets, bringing forth the end of The Beatles (a cultural phenomenon) and the end of hippy idealism that helped to adjust humanity's mindset. These two forces always seem to create beginnings and endings within a cycle of astrological movements. What we can deduce is that within the context of the future, when these two are in major aspect, a certain shift in our lives needs to happen internally and externally. In the natal charts of countries, Jupiter and Saturn become the strength of the moment; this means that without a strong Jupiter (idealism) and Saturn (structure) it is very difficult for that country to function under the energy and influence of the rest of the planets.

If we want the ability to look at future cycles of this world and indeed the universe, we must look towards individual countries to judge possible outcomes. Each country has its own natal chart according to when that nation was given a governmental structure or independence. This is what is called Mundane Astrology, which looks at the cycles of the planets in relation to each individual country's natal chart. In turn, each mundane natal chart has twelve segments that correlate to a particular aspect of how a country is run and what areas within those twelve segments are affected. Below is a list of the twelve houses and what each house signifies in terms of a country's function.

The First House Ascendant

This is perhaps the most important house within the natal chart, for it is the 'self-image' that we present to the world. For example, in the UK we have Libra on the first house cusp, which contributes to our need for balance and proper manners. We take great pride in how we appear as a country and the Venus influence has always made us appear to be rather good in the creative arts, music and literature. Sagittarius is the sign that is rising in the east at the time 1776, and we can clearly see the optimistic approach of the 'American Dream' symbolised in the making of a Sagittarius rising. France has Aries rising in the first house, contributing to the hot-headed passionate approach of the ram's energy. It is how other countries view a country and how that country views itself; the first house is the initial appearance of a nation. If we take the idea of a conception of a country then this is the starting point that the eleven other houses follow.

The Second House

The conception is embedded, now it is time for the country to create and build for its inhabitants. The point of the second house is to survive through material resources; money comes under the umbrella of the second house, as do financial institutions and banks in general. Without these in place a nation is unable to supply its needs and produce for other countries. This is the house of building on solid foundations.

The Third House

The house of communication and trade, this house also rules schools, journalism, technology (like the internet), telecommunications, the postal service, television and the language of the nation. For a county to evolve it has to expand its levels of how it communicates outside of itself. It is the third house that gives an indicator of how a nation does this.

The Fourth House IC

The base of society comes under rulership in the fourth house; this includes the home environment and the industry of agriculture, the seeds of time, or put in a simpler way it is the roots of a nation. It is the house of the zodiac sign of Cancer and therefore it is the land or mother earth of the country – what we sow we reap.

The Fifth House

This is the house of creativity, where pleasure and enjoyment come into the equation of a nation. Music, art, theatre and the romance of a country all come under the rulership of the fifth house. It also rules children, how we respond to them and ultimately treat them. Financial speculation and gambling is also under the rays of the fifth house, as well as the 'drama' of a society.

The Sixth House

Work and service provide the energy for the sixth house of a nation: rules, regulations, health and safety, councils, and the health service. The nature is of the zodiac sign of Virgo, which is ruled by Mercury.

The Seventh House Descendant

This is fundamentally the relationship house, and is related to allies as well as societies in general; it is the house of partnerships. The so-called 'special' relationship between the UK and the US would be seen in the seventh house in both natal charts. Justice and the legal system also come under this Libran house. Enemies who are known are situated in this house.

The Eighth House

International finance and other nations' money is under the eighth house. It is also the house of death and therefore it is how a nation deals with death. Included too are taxes, cycles in rebirth and a country's attitude towards sex, and how the country views sexual relations and taboos.

The Ninth House

Here we have the higher education, adult colleges and universities; also spirituality, religion, political views, long-distance communication and the philosophy of a nation. Our identity can be wrapped up in our religious and moral codes. The ninth house also covers long-distant travel and the overseas affairs of the government.

The Tenth House MC

This is the house of ambition. If the fourth house is the root of the country, then the tenth house is the branches that reach out, expanding and developing. So this house is the ruler of governments and the Royal Family; it is the basis of society including 'class systems'.

The Eleventh House

This is the house of hopes, dreams and wishes; but also fears. It is the collective house and therefore can indicate how a country is 'feeling' and what it is expecting. Local government and how we elect also come under this house.

The Twelfth House

This is the house of the hidden; it rules hospitals, monasteries, mental institutions, prisons and boarding schools. Secret societies and the general occult are ruled by this house. The twelfth house's other title is the house of self-undoing, and perhaps more than any other house it directs where a country's karma is shown.

The houses are portals that the planets manipulate and 'work through', shining a light on areas that need to be dealt with. When looking at a country's chart (we will do so in the next chapter) we determine which planets rule which houses. In viewing a chart and looking at the cycles of that chart, we need to know the influences that are in place already that will be positive or negative depending on their placements. As we have seen, each country has its own natal chart, just as each individual has its own birth chart; this is constructed at a moment when a government is elected or a country becomes united as in the case with the UK, when it linked in with Scotland, Northern Ireland and Wales in 1801. Astrology fundamentally is all about time and moments within time. Of course time is a concept that is man-made, it gives structure and supports a framework that we can work alongside. But the concept is dictated by our relationship with the cycles of the Sun and Moon and the seasons. This is the basic construction of time and indeed astrology, for the zodiac is based around the seasons, with the spring equinox being the start and finish. This is a function that is to do with nature's rhythm and humanity's ability to live and survive within that rhythm. Agriculture teaches us how to live within our means; this means that the planting of a seed (this can also represent an idea) followed by the right nurturing can bring things to fruition for us. In other words our direct link with the earth supplies us with answers. Astrology works within this framework of seasonal cycles, rather than the constellations which scientifically have changed over the centuries. Therefore astrology is very much fixed with the earth, and is grounded just as much with the trees as with the stars. So with astrology the astrologer in the case of horary astrology picks a moment in time, or nature does, as in the case of when a child is born. Within that moment it is as if a photograph is taken of the planets' positions and aspects, and that time encapsulates an individual's or a group's energies that are supportive, and also the challenges that must be learnt. However, within that fixed moment (which is the backdrop to the person or event) the planets still rotate around the Earth and hit sensitive points within the original natal chart. This determines cycles within a chart, for example you have the inner wheel (the moment of birth, the event) and the outer wheel (the activities of the planets within the past, present and future). So there is a dynamic force that operates between energies within a moment in time and with what is occurring at another moment. The basis of this is slightly abstract; however, as humans we are made up of moments within our own consciousness and patterns that are taken from our past. Moments within our life can become catalysts for change: a love affair, a job change, redundancy, health matters, marriage, children, death or even a spiritual awakening. This collection of major events imprints on our personality and helps to create a larger and more rounded individual based on our experiences and our responses. The same hypothesis is valid for a moment or an event for a country, as major events (internal or external) can have a profound effect on a country's identity and its behaviour as a collective.

Chapter 5

England's Dreaming
Johnny Rotten, 1977

To demonstrate how astrology works within a given framework, I am now going to look in detail at the energies of the UK's natal chart. The chart that you see below is taken from the coming into force of the Union of Great Britain and Ireland 1/1/1801 00.00LT.

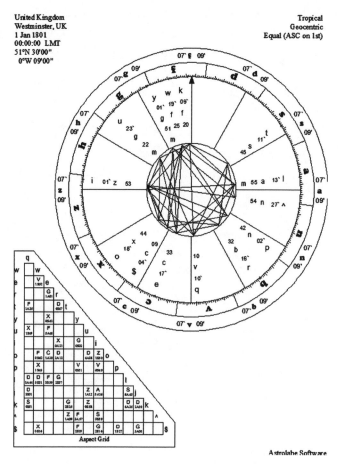

The natal chart for the United Kingdom is taken from when Britain joined up with its neighbours, including Northern Ireland. There are other charts for the UK, but after much study of the cycles, the 1801 in my opinion gives a better indicator of major events that fit in with the energies and placements of the planets. The first aspect to study is the influence of the sign that was travelling over the eastern point of the horizon. Within the context of the UK's chart this is placed in the Venus-ruled Libran zodiac sign. This deals with the myth and image of the UK; it is our mask to the world and how other countries view us. The idea of the UK being a nation of fair-minded people who are cultured (Venus) but who remain emotionally restrained (air) is revealed in the Libran ascendant coupled with Uranus in the twelfth house, making a wide conjunction to the ascendant. This is a mark that again plays out the 'English eccentric', for Uranus is not known for following the crowd. Uranus also makes a sextile aspect to Jupiter, increasing the need we have to express ourselves in different ways. Jupiter is placed in the tenth house in the equal house system, ruling public opinion. There is also an internal battle within the UK, as the south node in Libra marks our energy, as we try to push ourselves forward as an individual country. Actually still needing support from others, relations with allies can then become clouded and strained within the course of history.

If the Libran ascendant reveals our mask, then the Sun in Capricorn reveals our national identity. Capricorn is the zodiac sign that rules work, and it is no surprise that the UK is known as a country with a strong work ethic. It is also a conventional sign that perhaps leans more towards conservative opinions rather than liberal ones. I am not referring to political parties, but merely an idea or credence. The Sun makes a strong trine aspect with Mars (placed in the eighth house of death and rebirth) while the Sun is in the fourth house; both houses are water and contribute to a need to establish firm security roots (fourth house) through strong convictions (eighth house). The trine aspect flows with positive energy, therefore as a nation we are able to transform the destructive (eighth house) and recreate (fourth house Sun) to bring about structure (Capricorn Sun). The two World Wars of the twentieth century are a good example of how these two planets work well in terms of a powerful rebirth in our own consciousness as a nation. However the Sun in the UK's chart also makes a strong opposition to our MC (which rules governmental institutions). This brings about a tense aspect that denotes a conflict between what we need (fourth house) and what we want (MC tenth house Cancer). It is as if the UK is at odds with itself, which probably contributes to a lot of creative energy but also gives us a sense of separation between the government and the people that it represents. However, there can also be a tremendous drive for power and authority with this aspect. The UK has this grand bearing on other countries, encapsulated in the quote 'Great Britain' which demonstrates its intention and its pompous attitude. This attitude is typical of the tense aspect between the Sun and MC. The Sun also makes a square aspect with the ascendant, making the image (first house) a contradiction to the identity (Sun) of the nation. How we want to be seen by the rest of the world might not be how the rest of the world sees us. The Libran ascendant is calm, diplomatic, charming, intelligent, balanced and giving to striking up partnerships, but the rest of the world might see the UK as ambitious, conservative, cold, money-minded, bossy and rather old-fashioned, as directed by the Sun in Capricorn. The Moon reflects our nurturing ability and also more mundane matters, such as how the UK deals with domestic affairs. The Moon in the UK's chart is in the sign of Cancer, the zodiac sign traditionally ruled by the Moon. It is also placed in the tenth house; the Moon rules the masses, making a democratic government. The Moon also rules the idea of family and roots (fourth house) while the tenth is very much under the rulership of the Royal Family; the two play a major part in the identity of the nation. The drama of the royals gives us entertainment as directed by Venus in the fifth house. The Moon's aspects are also revealing as the UK has a Moon inconjunct with Mercury, giving rise to the media and gossip about people in the public eye (Moon tenth house). Mercury is placed in the third house of communications in Sagittarius. The UK's media exports travel far and wide under the guidance of Sagittarius. The third house is the house of Gemini which rules publishing and education, two areas that the UK has dominated not only in its own country but also abroad (Sagittarius). The Moon also makes a flowing trine aspect to the planet of illusion (Neptune) which is placed in the second house in Scorpio. The UK has seen tremendous success with film and theatre (Neptune) and of course music; on a cultural basis in history this has put the UK at a centre point (Moon tenth house conj. MC). The Moon in Cancer and in the tenth house is a melting pot for popularity and the aspect to Neptune signifies activity within the context of the arts, and being able to make money from it (Neptune second house). The public then receives this energy and becomes defensive (Cancer) and proud (tenth house) when under attack. Culture has always been closely associated with the UK, and the way in which a nation deals with culture, including music, fashion, writing, theatre and in general the aspects of social activity, is all explored through the planet Venus. In the UK's natal chart, Venus is placed in the zodiac sign of Aquarius in the Leo fifth house. Venus in Aquarius adds certain glamour and unconventionality to proceedings. One example is that the UK (in the western world) has become a benchmark for unusual fashion statements. France (another country that is known for its association with fashion) has Venus in the sign of Libra, in other words stylish, chic and very balanced in appearance. However, the UK's Venus in Aquarius is a little more daring; think of the Punk Movement, and the swinging sixties, and the unusual designs that were either inspired by the past (sixties fashion had a link with Victorian aspects) or directed to the future (the new romantic period) – both ideals are very Aquarian in principle. Mercury is in strong sextile aspect to Venus, allowing Venus' energy to be advocated and explored (Sagittarius third house) to other nations. The fifth house themes of creativity, children, gambling and romance fit in with the literature of Shakespeare, D.H. Lawrence, E.M. Forster, and even Mills and Boon and Barbara Cartland. The principle energy is unrequited love, or the romantic ideal of love, played out in the fifth house. The other planet that is situated in this house is Pluto; however, this is in the sign of Pisces. Pluto was not discovered at the conception of this UK's natal chart. I am inclined to only use its energy within the time that Pluto was discovered, ie 1930. Since that period there has been an explosive amount of creativity and spirituality within the UK, a direct result from the Second World War, again the idea of rebirth that is always a theme when Pluto is evident. The sign of Pisces is about endings since it is the sign at the end of the zodiac and the season. Pisces is about shifting boundaries and revealing new insights through a cloud of abstract thought. The fact that Pluto is in 2 degrees of Pisces is symbolically about balance with the masculine and the feminine. In trying to reach that ideal (Pisces) a transformation (Pluto) has to occur, which can be ongoing and cyclical in its movement within the idea of creativity. So where does Pluto fit in with this all? Pluto in Pisces is constantly shifting the boundaries of the nation's creativity, it helps to challenge perceptions and literally turn things upside down. However, it can cause misunderstandings and scandals that clearly have sexual overtones; this is a very acute problem with public figures in the UK. Saturn is the planet that exposes structure and limitations; it can add stability but can also cause slowness in economic growth. In the UK's chart it is placed in the royal sign of Leo, in the eleventh house of Aquarius. Its position is 23 degrees, a symbol of Mercury and assigned to that planet in the Arian decant. There is a nervous energy with Saturn at this degree that marks a tipping point from the tried and tested (Saturn) to the dramatic (Leo). The aspects that Saturn makes with other planets in the chart reveal more. Saturn makes an opposition (if a bit weak) with Venus. Again this emphasises the juxtaposition of the conventional and the rather bohemian attitude in the nation's consciousness. The push and pull of this aspect can get things moving but can also at times create a 'stuck in a rut' syndrome that needs shaking up. Saturn will also impose a limit on things and its aspect to Venus reinforces that, so that we get the Venus expression through the arts, and then the structures are put into place to create a business (Saturn) from this expression, ie music, fashion, film (fifth house). Jupiter is high in the sky in the tenth house, giving rise and energy to the political arena of the UK's chart. It also makes a strong sextile to Uranus in the twelfth house, which surely would indicate the equality and humanitarian instincts within the National Health Service (twelfth house). Jupiter's rays are beneficial and since the twelfth house rules hospitals, prisons and general places of recuperation or sacrifice, the government (tenth house) would support these institutions. The UK's chart shows a dominance of cardinal signs, meaning that it is a chart of action; the nation wants to pursue greatness and be a leader on the world stage. The two elements that are powerfully placed are fire and water signs; these two elements have an adverse effect on each other, water putting out the fire. So the UK can at times seem a little indecisive, accentuated by the Libran ascendant. The fixed signs of Taurus, Leo, Scorpio and Aquarius also dominate, creating a stubborn nation with plenty of aspects of squares and oppositions. It is by no means an easy chart for a nation, but then again it does have a very dynamic energy to it that revels in the pomp of its history and the 'kookiness' of its creativity.

The next eight years in the period 2012–2020 will see the UK challenged on all levels as it seeks to reinforce its morals and principles again on the world stage. In January 2012 transiting Pluto will make a strong conjunction with the UK's Sun in the fourth house (equal house system). This will put to the test our basic survival techniques and our foundations from the past. This is when past actions could come back to haunt us, especially in the area of the Middle East and the war on terror. The fourth house is also the place of endings, meaning our nurturing skills are questioned and reformed; remember Pluto is not a planet that bodes easily with compromise. The basic premise is one of diluting the 'ambition' and concentrating on the 'needs' of the country; it is with this that we can gain transformation and understanding through hardship and change. The agriculture of the country will also undergo a reformation leading to a new type of farming and education that will help the UK to rebuild an industry using the land. This will take time but the ethos should start to manifest during early 2012. Uranus in Aries travels through the UK's sixth house, the house of service, and on a more fundamental level, work and industry. Uranus over the next year will go back and fourth over the UK's descendant, causing an anarchic energy in relation to our allies and the world stage perception of the UK in its judgements and past collaborations. The destabilising influence of Pluto and Uranus will make 2012 a very hard year indeed. The Olympics in London in the summer of 2012 will be activated when Uranus is exact 7 degrees on the Aries ruled by Mars (sport) descendant opposing the UK's Libran ascendant. This causes strife but also an unpredictable energy, causing trouble through protest and in the transport systems; it is as if the Olympics will prove to be too much for London to deliver in terms of its people. It is the people (who ordinarily live in London) who will feel the most stifling energies of the event. Saturn will also square the natal Moon, the ruler of the fourth house (Pluto's temporary home), governing the tenth house of institutions and the government. For the UK, this is the beginning of the crisis point, because Pluto is transiting in an angle house and Uranus is at a angle point, the descendant; this means that the unconsciousness (fourth house) and the viewpoints of others (seventh house descendant) are being subjected to a grilling on a national level. As we go into the year 2013, Pluto is at 10 degrees Capricorn which is exactly on the UK's natal Sun 10 degrees in Capricorn. This also opposes the UK's MC causing a shift in priorities that could have implications for future governments. The question of function will be how the masses are controlled when weakness in the current government have been exposed, causing the first signs of an uprising in the political arena. Neptune, the planet of illusion, transits the UK's natal Pluto, and the conjunction aspect is formed, a potent energy that causes scandals and misunderstandings. Within the UK's chart it is revealed in the fifth house of creativity and children, and this may lead to the first open debates and scientific ideas regarding the genetic engineering of children. The obsession with youth will continue, and creative movements in the theatre (Pisces) will begin to flourish as the youth (fifth house) demand more tangible forms of art that use all of the physical senses. However, there could also be a drive to dominate immediate surroundings; the UK's freedom of speech (under a democratic government) could lead to an overbearing presence in other countries' political systems. Neptune will always cloud issues so that the receivers of Neptune's energies can get confused with the messages that they are channelling. The contact with Pluto will only intensify matters that come under the house it occupies, the fifth in this case. By July, Jupiter will oppose the UK's natal Sun, revealing the stress that the country has been experiencing over the last eighteen months. However, an opposition is by no means easy and it could reflect a time of over-optimism on the government's part. This could lead to the making of disastrous decisions in spending policies.

However, by the autumn Jupiter is in the tenth house and Saturn is in the UK's second house, and this is a crucial time for the UK to deal with financial issues instead of overseas matters. Here, lessons from the past will help to steer them in the right direction. In terms of 'points' in an astrological sense, ie in regard to a natal chart, the UK reaches that crisis 'point' in 2014, as Pluto still transits the natal Sun, Uranus goes back over the descendant and Saturn comes into contact with natal Neptune in the second house by conjunction. The outer planets at sensitive points in a chart cause external changes to occur in the nation's consciousness, and 2014 is one of those occasions. The response from humanity has to be in line with the events that occur at this point. What I mean is that our need to rebuild the structures of the UK's society will be strong with ideas coming in from people born with Neptune in Sagittarius, from the early 1970's till 1984. This generation will have a broader outlook and will be much more philosophical in their thinking processes, which is a real contrast to the previous generation who were born with Neptune in Scorpio, meaning motivations were through self-examination rather than outward participation. As the Neptune in Sagittarius generation reaches positions of power, inspiration will be sought to build a new society from the example of other cultures, as Neptune is far-reaching in its energy and Sagittarius is the arche-typal traveller of the zodiac. Transiting Saturn in aspect with natal Neptune is a good indicator of the trouble that could be caused for the UK. When these two planets meet it brings about worry because of the inconsistency of Neptune in the natal chart; Saturn's energy ignites the more vulnerable energies of Neptune, so that the planet is not allowed to drift into its own reality. Because Neptune is situated in the second house which rules the country's ability to gain and make money on a very basic level, Saturn is challenging the UK to be more frugal in its approach to finances. The conjunction between these two is symbolic of the headmaster who meets the artist to see what they can both create.

The UK in 2014 could be in for a very creative period in terms of exporting goods made in the UK to other countries, as Saturn likes to work and Neptune like to create. This would be the positive aspect of the meeting of these two planets; the negative would be a battle between these two planetary bodies that in the end creates nothing of any substance. Astrology is about how a country or an individual responds to the planets' energies. As the UK enters 2015 the planets especially on the angles are less intense than in 2014 but only momentarily. Jupiter will make a conjunction with the UK's natal Saturn in the eleventh house, allowing high ideals to materialise, which suggests that a new government will come into power during this period. Jupiter also forms an opposition with natal Venus, contributing to new forms artistically which express the UK's desires and issues through an aesthetic form. In April 2015 Saturn hits the UK's Chiron in Sagittarius, still in the second house and causes the country to reconsider how it makes it money. Chiron, the wounded healer, always wants to heal the past through accep-tance and forgiveness, so the UK will have to come to terms with the fact that it needs to create its own individual industry if it is to survive (second house) in the world market (Saturn). The year 2016 marks a time of recovery and moving forward from a period of great strain and hardship. Pluto opposes the natal Moon in 2016, creating problems with identity and also the health system and how the country looks after disadvantaged children. The Moon symbolises how a country looks after its society and how the UK functions as a whole. Pluto is a power-house planet which means that the government is not necessarily hit by the problems of the country directly, but that the general population (fourth house) and the emotional needs (Moon in Cancer) of the UK's population will be. However, by the autumn of 2016 Jupiter will start to pass over the ascendant in the UK's chart. This brings about the beginning of a new twelve-year cycle for the country. As Jupiter passes between the twelfth house (of karma) and the first house (of image), the UK can expect a period of fortitude going into 2017. Jupiter's rays are benevolent in energetic shifts and therefore can bring in a shift of optimism that will start to radiate from the country's consciousness. However, this will also aspect the UK's natal Uranus marking a period of great technological insight and advancement, but shifting changes in the country's world image, marking the Aquarian themes of brotherhood and sisterhood as they become a beacon of truth and ethos. For the rest of 2017 the mantra will be 'hard work pays your way', as opportunities start to manifest in industry with the use of natural fibres and an interest in sustainable living developing a job market for the masses. Because of Jupiter's cycle through the first house, in 2018 it will be in the UK's second house continuing the new structures that were implemented by governmental initiatives. Jupiter also activates natal Neptune signalling a time when the nation's ideals could get in the way of the reality of what has occurred in the economic situation during the last four years. When Jupiter and Neptune make contact an overemphasis on the 'God factor' comes into play. This means that we can become too faithful with the law of energy, so that we miss the details in our ideals. This is when Saturn comes into the forefront, supporting and engaging with Jupiter's and Neptune's energies. During this time period Saturn is slowly making a strong conjunction with the UK's natal Sun in Capricorn. The significance of this combination heralds a return to roots (fourth house) and a traditional approach to politics (Saturn) that unearths (Pluto) secrets from the UK's political past. In 2019 the country is stabilised by the entrance of Saturn into the fourth house still making an aspect with the natal Sun. Any planet that is on the angle, in this case the IC, signifies a reaction and direction to outside events. Saturn limits scope but also adds weight to argument, the control over the country's finances is at the root of the UK's agricultural and creative endeavours. As the year develops Saturn transits closely to transiting Pluto which symbolically causes power struggles and authoritarian issues. How the UK's government will deal with these energies is likely to bring about chaos or change that will benefit many. Because of the fourth house emphasis, which during the period 2012–2020 dominates the UK's chart, there is a direct opposition with the MC which is on the cusp of the tenth house (astrologically this is the Capricorn home). The axis between the fourth and tenth is an angle that in mundane astrology correlates to the motivation of a country and the inspirational aspects; when these two are activated by planets transiting it causes a revaluation of basic drives and principles. This means that there is no hiding place for the UK because whatever passes through the fourth house will naturally aspect the tenth house. Therefore you could say that the UK's unconscious objectives are more readily seen by the outer world, making the country more vulnerable to political mistakes that have no validation.

As the UK comes to the end of the year 2020, there is a close conjunction between Saturn and Pluto by 2 degrees. Uranus is now in the zodiac sign of Taurus with Neptune in the sixth which causes issues with the health system but also allows more alternative practices to become the norm. The outcome for the UK from the last eight-year cycle is one of momentous struggle and change for the government and the citizens of the UK.

Chapter 6

'I Have a Dream'
Martin Luther King, 1963

Understandably, the chart of the United States of America is different from the UK's chart. First of all it is dominated by the cardinal quality and the elements air and water are also very apparent. Air and water can cook up a storm if left too much to their own devices. The US' chart suggests this country is a great starter of new projects and ideas, but that it is not so good at sustaining them. The first aspect to look at in the chart is the ascendant sign which is the window that other countries 'look through', ie what they perceive the States to be. In the US' chart the ascendant sign is the mutable fire sign of the archer Sagittarius which is ruled by expansive Jupiter. This is a rather optimistic sign with the archer pointing its many arrows in the air to see where they land. This is very much the archetypal symbol for the US. In generalised terms America is seen as a land of opportunity (Sagittarius) that embeds its philosophy on the great American dream (Jupiter). It also can lead to rather impulsive action and religious convictions that can be rather dogmatic in their approach. The Sun of the US' chart is in the water sign Cancer, indicating a very different energy from the Sagittarian outlook. The Cancer Sun places a high degree of its resources on security and building a family network. It also depicts a rather secretive nature, and since the Sun is placed in the Scorpion eighth house, the need for the nation to keep tearing down old structures and rebuilding is evident. The Sun makes many aspects, two conjunctions (although weak in orb) to Venus and Mercury, bringing the need for communication and joviality (Jupiter conjunct Sun). The ruler of the Sun in Cancer, the Moon

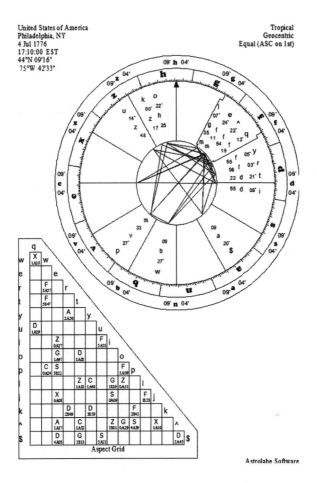

United States of America
Philadelphia, NY
4 Jul 1776
17:10:00 EST
44°N 09'16"
75°W 42'33"

Tropical
Geocentric
Equal (ASC on 1st)

Aspect Grid

Astrolabe Software

is in the forward-looking idealistic sign of Aquarius, which complements the Sagittarian ascendant. Situated in the third house of communication, publishing, education and technology, the States have made these aspects the height of their outlook and thinking. The Moon is in trine with Mars in Gemini, empowering this country with great powers of persuasion and gifting it with the ability to convey ideas in a straightforward way (Mars is placed in the seventh house, taking the lead in decisions). The ruler of the third house, Uranus, is significant in the US' chart; it is in conjunction with the descendant and its cycle seems to create great upheavals in the US' chart including the instigation of wars. The Uranus opposition to the ascendant causes an imbalance in how the US wants to be seen by the rest of the world, and the reality of how the nation is different from the image (ascendant). The rebellious nature of Uranus will always cause the US to be reckless in its actions and to think (Aquarius) that it is right in all it does. The nervous energy of Uranus in Gemini can be difficult to control and hard to ignore. Therefore an over-emphasis on the air element can at times cause the US' society to have its head in the clouds. However, the US is a nation of glamour and has the ability to create a separate reality. Where does that come from? The planet Neptune is high in the sky in the tenth house making a conjunction to its MC. This is the planet of inspiration and also rules films. The idealistic vibrations of Neptune are felt in the consciousness of the nation's dwellers but also on a worldwide scale. Neptune also makes a strong sextile aspect with Mercury, creating a unique essence to convert dreams into some kind of package that can be sold. Personalities and celebrities are given almost mythical status. Think of figureheads like Marilyn Monroe (Gemini), Jimi Hendrix (Sagittarius), J.F. Kennedy (Gemini), Martin Luther King (Capricorn), Barack Obama (Leo), Michael Jackson (Virgo), Madonna (Leo), Johnny Depp (Gemini). All seem to embody a optimistic and expansive (Jupiter) theme that has a particular reference to the Sagittarius virtues. The constant need to conquer and spread their ideals is in keeping with the Jupiter ethos. In the aspect of how the nation enjoys itself, and indeed all the social aspects of the country, we look to the planet Venus which in the US' chart is in the sign of Cancer. The sign of the crab is home-loving, enjoys eating, can be sentimental, with a strong conviction of family values and community. These themes seem to embody the US. Remember Cancer is a cardinal sign, it is not stagnant; it prefers to push itself forward and make its own rules. As the US grows in historical stature, I feel it would be safe to say that it could in its own collective unconscious become stuck in the past (Sun and Venus in Cancer) but these planets probably denote the friendliness that the nation is known for throughout the world. Mercury, the planet of communication, is also in Cancer in the eighth house, a potent combination for witty humour and a very psychological approach to the mind. Breaking new ground in these areas is something the United States seems to do with ease. Jupiter the ruler of the ascendant is also placed in Cancer, which gives the chart an over-emphasis on one sign. An over-dominance of the seventh and eighth houses combines to create a need to relate with others (seventh Libran house) and transform independently (eighth Scorpio house). This can lead to the issue of becoming involved in other countries' issues or a need (Cancer) to get involved in foreign countries' problems. If you think of an individual with a strong Cancer in their chart, you will see that they have a need to nurture, that also they may have issues with letting go of the past, may be over-emotional, sentimental, clingy and moody; these traits depict the phases of the Moon. These characteristics can be applied to a nation, or at least in their subconscious. Because the US has Cancer as a dominant sign in its chart it means that some of these characteristics are over-accentuated, pushing the country in a direction that it does not necessarily want to go (wars being one aspect). Pluto is placed in the second house in the sign of Capricorn at 27 degrees; the recent entrance of Pluto in Capricorn in 2008 will have a profound effect on the US' economy over the next twenty-four years, meaning that new ways of sustaining the financial market will have to be found. The second house rules financial survival and therefore how a country makes its money. Pluto at the time of conception in the second house gives great reserves of energy and ideas, but first the country needs to go through many trans-formations and rebirths before it can direct its 'power' in the right way. Abuse of this could lead to a need (Cancer) to exert power (Pluto) over other countries' economies (second house). Mercury also makes an opposition with Pluto causing miscommunications with other countries' money (eighth house). The North Node in Leo in the ninth house signifies expansion within the education system and foreign travel; there is certainly a need to learn lessons through how the States treats others, and these lessons can be hard. The South Node is in the third house, meaning that they find the basic idea of communicating and getting their point across rather easy, as if blessed with these skills.

The US' natal chart characterises the need for expansion and optimism that we associate with the country in terms of its own persona. The ruler of the chart is Jupiter, which looks for ways of expressing itself but also its relationship with other countries; this is in contradiction with the Cancer need to stay at home. This means that the States is in conflict with itself. The way in which we see the US is different from how they see themselves and therefore what you see is definitely not what you get. However, the planet Uranus is the planet that seems to have the biggest impact on the US, especially in relation to great changes and upheavals with political and social unrest. Because it is in the shadow aspect (the descendant) angle, the US has a tendency to try to hide the more violent and reactionary aspects of its consciousness as a country.

The year 2012 for the US promises to be a year when ideals will be discussed with passion and structure (Saturn travelling in the eleventh house). Saturn always likes to get serious when it comes to consuming energy. The eleventh house is the house of Aquarius and therefore idealistic principles will dominate the thoughts of the American government. The other major theme will be economy as Pluto the planet of transformation and under-ground activity will have just entered the US' second house (equal house system) in January 2012. The significance of this combination will be powerful because during the next eight years Pluto will remain in the second house uncovering the US' ability to make money from its own resources. Remember the symbolic image attached to Pluto is the Phoenix rising from the ashes. The economic situation can be revitalised under the guidance of Pluto if it is allowed to literally clear out the clutter of old rules and regulations. However, if Pluto is restrained in any way it becomes the destroyer. The second house also becomes one of the most important houses in mundane astrology for it is the house of basic survival, how a country creates; it is the house of Taurus which 'wants' to build firm foundations for the future. The US will have to use the energy of Pluto wisely; the implications of not doing so could reveal the hidden underworld in the US therefore exposing fraud and embezzlement that would embarrass the US' government. Pluto does not tread carefully and anything that needs to be exposed will be, under its influence. In the US' natal chart Pluto rules the twelfth house or as it is rather traditionally expressed, 'the house of self-undoing'. Karmic debt is paid under the direct rays of the twelfth house and because the ruler of that house is in the second, the US' economic market will have to dig deep to be able to pay back what they have metaphorically taken. The North Node is in conjunction with the US' ascendant in Sagittarius, meaning that the US has the capability of reinventing its image on the world stage. This is also reinforced by an opposition aspect to the US' natal Sun, which in January 2012 is exactly filtering through the degree of eight, a number ruled by the planet Saturn. Hard work will be expected by all as the battle between the zodiac signs of Cancer and Capricorn pushes domestic and work issues to the forefront of the political agenda. Uranus also enters a new home as it enters the fifth house, enabling creative expression, a reaction to the heaviness of Pluto. This will make the artistic movement of music the central theme for the US' youth movement, so that we have a similar sub-culture from the grunge music of the early nineties. The year of 2013 breathes a certain sense of optimism as Jupiter enters the sign of Cancer (the

Sun sign in the US' chart). Jupiter takes a usual orbit of twelve months to complete a cycle through one zodiac sign. Jupiter will predominantly be passing through the US' eighth house which rules Scorpio, again putting the emphasis on the Pluto factor. Both the UK and the US are during this period under major influences from the planet Pluto so perhaps significantly their ethos of the 'war on terror' will become a noose around their necks. However, Jupiter is powerfully placed because it marks the time of the US' Jupiter return; this is when a planet transiting makes a conjunction aspect with the same planet in the natal chart. The Jupiter return marks a period when efforts from the past bear fruit in the present, and it can also mark a period of great rewards. In the mundane chart of the US the ruler of the eighth house is the Moon, which is placed in the third house in Aquarius. This symbolises great advancement in relation to communication, media and education. The need to restructure the US' education system will be strong, creating a new way of dealing with economic issues in the future. The year 2013 will see a marked shift in polices and exporting educational ideas and this will give the US a new focal point for its intentions over the next eight years.

2014 kicks into action as Saturn travels through the US' twelfth house. Saturn is now at the end of its cycle and is therefore in the twelfth to clean up the undercurrents of the nation's collective unconsciousness. During the period of early 2014 Mars contacts the natal Moon; this causes a fire and water combination that generates some turbulent decisions with emotional (Moon) objectives (Mars). During early 2013 Saturn makes a trine aspect to the natal Sun in Cancer, allowing the more humanitarian instincts to come to the surface. As the US goes into the year 2014 Jupiter makes an exact aspect to the natal Sun; it is at this time that the US begins to find its feet again in terms of direction. Uranus also squares the natal Sun, energising but also creating tension that manifests in a high intensity of commercial output commercial. The economic tide is turning for the US as a new world view is being formed for the country as a whole.

The year 2015 is in stark contrast to the previous year. Transiting Neptune, the planet of illusion, forms a strong square with the US' ascendant. Any contact between Neptune and the ascendant questions and challenges the area of identity. The first house represents the image of a country and how that country presents itself to the rest of the world. Neptune seeks a union with something beyond the ordinary. Neptune in early 2015 is positioned in the late degrees of the thrid house. This means that in 2015 it will enter the fourth house which is an angular house and one of prime importance. Because the ascendant is in the zodiac sign of Sagittarius, there is automatically the need for the US to portray itself as overtly optimistic, mainly because of the positive ruler of the chart Jupiter. It would be safe to assume that the indicators of this combination are that the US will bite off more than it can chew. The reasoning behind this is that Jupiter is strong during the year 2015 in its chart, as is Neptune; therefore these two planets can literally seek salvation and redemption through the power of positive thought or religious objectives, becoming dogmatic in their approach. The world can seem scary and lack direction; therefore Jupiter and Neptune symbolise a 'meaning' and union through the power of the God form. This energy is so strong during 2015 that the US is in danger of becoming all-consumed in creating a society in which moralistic principles are formed from a deep need to connect to a higher form. Not that this is a bad thing; in fact you could say that it enables societies to move on to another level of consciousness. However, the question is to what extent will the rest of the world sympathise with the US' new-found salvation? The answer may lie in the year 2016 when Saturn passes over the US' ascendant causing a very grounding and realistic experience.

Saturn is now at the start of a new cycle and wants to put right what went wrong. The North Node also makes an exact aspect to the natal Neptune, and this coupled with Saturn's energies brings conflict, the pragmatic is in an argument with the illusionist. The US will feel tested at this time and many governmental scandals could come to the surface over this twelve-month period, as Neptune never keeps secrets for long. Transiting Jupiter is also at the same degree angle of 22 degrees in January 2016; the meaning of 22 degrees is the overthrow of established patterns that brings about more stability. The number two is related to the Moon and two plus two makes four, which in numerology is ruled by the planet Uranus. The US is going to have to be very careful if it becomes involved in any revolutions outside of its own country during 2016. The energies that are firing on all cylinders can cause a destabilisation and what is termed in this book as a 'crisis point'. Pluto is still situated in the second house for the US and therefore is still dredging up aspects of the US' underworld that the government would rather not come out in public. The prison system will come under review and this includes how criminals are treated in terms of the ethics of the 'system'. By the time that 2017 comes along the US should feel the pressure that everyone is under and in some ways more. Uranus transiting makes a close contact as the US' natal, Chiron (the wounded healer of the asteroids) comes knocking at the door of Uranus, bringing disruption through relations with other countries. Aries is the ruler of the fifth house and Mars the ruler is placed in the seventh house of partnerships. The US during this time will certainly have a clear idea who its enemies are. But because of the Uranus factor, the normal rules of engagement might not apply as they did in the past. This may put the US on the defensive during 2017 and in 2018, in fact they may feel a need to psychologically retreat from the world stage although Uranus and Pluto will always want to push them further into the spotlight. As 2018 begins to edge through, Neptune lingers around the bottom of their chart near the IC. It follows that the roots of their political substance are based on judgements that do not have enough realistic expectations; this could lead to a breakdown and confusion in regard to land owners and could affect mortgages between the government and the general American population. Chiron also opposes the natal Neptune causing real issues in regard to social reforms and health proposals. The US could find that their own citizens rebel against the wishes of the government, because of bad communication. As the US enters the year 2019, the planets seem to settle into a much more stable vibration. Jupiter travels through the first house and into the second, beginning a new cycle that helps the US to start to solidify its results from an economic point of view. In January 2020 transiting Mars will be in Sagittarius over the US' ascendant; this is an important point, because the identity of the country will be one of renewed confidence and direction. Jupiter, Saturn and Pluto are also situated in the second house, helping to build and create new industries that will boost the US' economy. The year 2020 will be a powerful year for the US, because it will bring a real sense of opportunism for the general population.

Chapter 7

The Structure of the Zodiac

The astrological zodiac is the template for the planets to work through but also react with, so that an energetic shift occurs. If the planets are the drivers, then the zodiac signs are the vehicles. They form the basis of the cycles of time that is such an important part of how the future is shaped and of what we can expect from the planets' transits. The zodiac is based on the seasons, less from the constellation (in western astrology) and therefore we can pinpoint what stage a planet is currently going through in its own cycle.

Aries

The Sun goes into the sign of Aries on the spring equinox on the 20th and 21st of March. This is when a new cycle has sprung, the energy when the Sun is in the zodiac sign of Aries is a time of new beginnings. Aries is a fire sign and therefore any planet that is situated or travelling through this sign is going to be either exaggerated or dampened; take the example of the planet Neptune in Aries, last seen in the middle of the nineteenth century. Aries is an energy that wants to be daring and wants to conquer new lands and find new ways of experiencing life; it is a competitive energy. We get results in the Aries way through drive and determination. For example, the need to escape from the dark winter months is a characteristic of Aries, for the sign is about the immediate future, and from the end of the cycle of Pisces (which is still embedded in the memory of Aries), the ram signals its intent of starting new projects and ideas that use the new energy of the Sun. The planets' relationship with this sign is one of bringing a far more direct approach to life; it is not sentimental but can be emotional in a childish way, the word 'selfish' is often attached to the zodiac sign of Aries. However, the selfish action of Aries helps to get things moving. We are at the start of a new cycle and just as when a baby is born into this world there is a need to experience as much as possible in order to gather knowledge in a physical sense.

Taurus

The second sign of the zodiac has a different energy from the previous sign (Aries). We are now firmly situated in the month of May, when fertility is celebrated and the earth is ripe for planting. The zodiac sign that is governing this period is Taurus with the symbol of the bull, demanding stability and nurturing of the land. Agriculture is attached to the sign of Taurus, and during the month of May the days become longer and flowers and plants come into in full bloom. Therefore any planet that is placed in Taurus will need to get results and find stability. Taurus is an unmovable force; being an earth sign and fixed in element, the need to build and create 'something' for the future is an important psychological gateway for the Taurus' energy. Any planet needs to learn the lesson of building for the future. We can think of the Age of Taurus (4000–2000 BC), which is directly related the Egyptians and their cultural society (Taurus is ruled by Venus) and their need to build (pyramids). However, the energy of Taurus can also become too bogged down and stagnant causing a rigid (earth, fixed) need to stick with what has been done before, that is if we stay in the Taurean period for too long. For example, Jupiter travelling in Taurus can increase our ability to create from the land, and it can also allow us to indulge (Jupiter) in our senses (Taurus).

Gemini

In Taurus we build and in Gemini we experience the need to communicate and express ourselves verbally. The symbol for the zodiac sign of Gemini is of the twins. This is a very human sign that embodies the challenge of always looking for that perfect match with which to communicate. Gemini is an air sign and so it needs to keep the circulation flowing, with ideas, writing, inventing or education. The need to challenge the mind and learn how things have been done in the past is high under the influence of Gemini. Italy is a country whose Sun is in Gemini as is South Africa. The constant need, similar to Aries, to move forward is strong; however, Aries is more direct than Gemini, the twins tend to spread themselves rather too thin. Gemini is a mutable sign and therefore is able to adapt to changes in circumstances. The heat of June burns bright in the zodiac sign of Gemini, and the butterfly is perhaps the perfect example of the energy of this sign. Once we have built (Taurus) the need to talk and exchange ideas is needed for the expansion of what we have conquered (Aries).

Cancer

The home becomes the mantra for the sign of Cancer, for without a home we have nothing to nurture and grow. Cancer is symbolised by the crab, a creature that carries its home wherever it goes. The need to find that sanctuary is an important psychological aspect of this sign because without that 'home' the Cancer can be at a loss, not finding its true identity. Once we have communicated (Gemini) the impetus is to settle down and begin to create the future through the family unit (Cancer). The US is dominated by the sign of Cancer in its chart and family values are important and challenged (from their natal Uranus) within the structures of their society. However, Cancer is a cardinal sign and therefore is a force in its own right; it has direction, and it signifies the need to protect, nurture and survive. The sign of Cancer is ruled by the Moon, a planet that is at best fluctuating in its energy and feminine in principle. But it is positive in its approach, for the cycle of Cancer is there to make sure that the foundations of the 'home' (meaning the society of a country in general) are well governed and given an opportunity to flourish.

Leo

We now come to the royal sign of Leo. It demands attention; it is symbolised by the constellation with the Lion, King of the jungle and is fiery in its nature. Ruled by the Sun, it is a sign of vitality and creativity; worshiped by millions, the Sun's rays are there to bring joy and fruitful times. The month of August is associated with the sign of Leo, when we are coming to the end of the summer months. The Sun burns bright and lingers as we bask in its glory; think of holidays that are mainly taken at this time. Planets are activated and re-energised under the influence of Leo, and there is an added need to express ourselves in colourful ways. Because of the fire element of the sign, Leo coupled with the fixed quality means that the intense beams of energy that are directed can overshadow deeper issues that normally go unnoticed – too much on the outward, not enough on the inward! Planets have a need to use this energy but can be rather dominating in the way that they use the rays of the Sun. However, the Sun begins to diminish in its power as we travel towards the end of the month; what is created from the past can now bear fruit. But it is now too late to start (Aries) new projects.

Virgo

The month of September comes into play for the zodiac sign of Virgo, as we reap the rewards of our efforts in harvest time. Virgo is symbolised by the maiden; another human sign, it is ruled by the planet Mercury, as is Gemini, the planet of communication. Our need is strong at this time to make sure that metaphorically our 'garden of Eden' is well-nourished and looked after for future springs and summers. The maiden is the worker. She cultivates a pure understanding of the Earth and the cosmos, and any planet that travels through Virgo is used to help humans understand human nature as well as the cycles that we have to undergo to reach illumination and understanding. Virgo is an esoteric key, for without the night (autumn equinox when the Sun passes from Virgo to Libra) we are stuck in a repetitive cycle, which needs to be shifted.

Libra

The scales are the symbol for Libra, and the word most closely associated with this sign is *balance*. Libra is an air sign that directs its energy with mental agility; so, in the great cycle of the zodiac we are back to communication, but this time within the structure of partnerships, how we cooperate with others and our diplomatic self. Libra is also a cardinal sign; it is given to 'action' and seeks to activate ideas through and with another, be it a person or in this case another country as depicted in the mythical alliance of the 'special relationship' between the UK and the US. The month is October and the nights begin to deepen and draw closer; it is the festival of 'Samian' or to give it its more commercial title, Halloween. This is when the veil between this earthly world and the 'other' world or dimensions are closely entwined, more in keeping with the next zodiac sign of Scorpio.

Scorpio

The mystical, sexual union of mind and emotions is at its peak in the underworld of Scorpio, ruled by the powerful and unrelenting energy of Pluto. This is a time to dig deeper into human issues. We have explored and conquered (Aries), built (Taurus), communicated (Gemini), settled and procreated (Cancer), basked in our glory (Leo), nurtured our past efforts (Virgo), and formed alliances and partnerships (Libra). Now it is time to delve into the deeper meaning of our own existence. Through the sign of Scorpio we are able to do this, to uncover truths and unlock the secrets of the universe through a connection, but with what? A person through sexual love, or a God of union, or the mind and its inner complexities? All of these facets, in fact, because Scorpio is all about transformation. Within this exploration a greater understanding can occur that helps humanity to reach its goals. Scorpio is a water sign and is fixed in nature; it wrestles with this juxtaposition, because its nature is basically turbulent. Therefore planets tend to react strongly through this zodiac sign, because there is no other way to 'react' and respond to the energy of Scorpio.

Sagittarius

We now have a different energy from the previous sign, less intoxicating in its presence. The sign of Sagittarius is symbolised by the archer (half-man, half-beast) and these qualities can be seen in the nature and energetic pull of this sign. The planet that rules the archer is the benevolent planet Jupiter. Sagittarius is a fire sign signalling a time of renewed energy and creative force. December in the western world is known as the party season and is the time ruled by Jupiter, a planet of indulgence. This is a time of optimism, a period when growth happens once more. The nights are now at their peak as the winter solstice on the 21st unites us with the cycle of winter, but before that happens we must rejoice and count our blessings as the Sun passes through Sagittarius.

Capricorn

We are now at the point of winter when we withdraw and cultivate our need for survival (we are back to the opposite sign of Cancer). But this time we have the harsh winter cold and barren landscape to contend with. The symbol for Capricorn is the goat; we are back to the animal signs (like Aries, Taurus and Leo) and the need to push forward and use determination to gain success is apparent as the goat has to make a journey up to the mountain to gain riches. Capricorn is ruled by the planet Saturn, the planet of the worker. We have celebrated and indulged under Sagittarius, now we must work and stick to the traditional; this is not a time to take risks, for the land does not support us all, there is barely enough to go round. However, if we maintain progress we can achieve great results, for Capricorn is a cardinal sign and it wants to push forward and reward our efforts.

Aquarius

The cold crisp air bites into the bones, but this is to remind us that we are humans who must strive for each other and work together. Capricorn is solitary in its motivation, while Aquarius, the sign of the water bearer, is brotherly in its approach. The Aquarius brings back lost knowledge from the past and wants everyone to be treated as equal; we begin to experience the more spiritual aspects of our consciousness. But this approach is different from Scorpio's which focuses on the internal to find its source. It (Aquarius) is an energy that looks externally to the past and to the future. Technology and advancement in how we interact with the world around us is on the agenda. The governmental structures that were put in place under the guidance of Capricorn are now dropped and the need is born for brotherhood and one morality. The idealistic nature of Aquarius ruled by the unpredictable planet of Uranus can cause problems in how we implement these new standards; it is now the time of a slow (fixed) and violent (Uranus) revolution. The Aquarius energy is full of hope for the possibilities of the future and it understands that in order to bring those changes about, the old structures have to go.

Pisces

We now come to the end of the cycle with the zodiac sign of Pisces, represented and symbolised by the two fishes swimming in different directions. Pisces is ruled by the nebulous planet of Neptune which rules fantasy and illusion. We have sacrificed so much to get this far in our evolution, yet the message is clear: beyond the physical are other dimensions and our entrance into these realms will be a totally different experience. The more spiritual aspects come under the spotlight under Pisces; however, this is different from the previous sign of Aquarius, for the Pisces cycle seeks to be united with the other world, or a godly form. This leads us to transcend our vision and spirituality to access another level, and to raise the vibrations of humanity. However, Pisces is a water sign and mutable in essence; it needs space and emotion (water) to fully engage with the higher realms. So our zodiac cycle comes to an end, and we either leave this earth or the cycle begins again. The last cycle allows the winter to merge with the spring; it is our last stage of development. Pisces is always about endings and the light just within reach, just as how when the Sun goes down the Moon arrives helping us to enter into the nocturnal night where darkness covers the boundaries that are created by the Sun.

The zodiac is the backbone to astrology; it shows what evolution and stage we are at as humans and which planet is activating that period, and whether it is positive or negative. Any outer planet (namely Jupiter, Saturn, Uranus, Neptune and Pluto) that enters the zodiac sign of Aries is at the start of a major new cycle, and this the same for Pisces, which is at the end. Therefore we must look at how the planet has dealt with this aspect in the past within the context of its journey through the zodiac.

Chapter 8

Aspects and their Meanings

An aspect is the energy created by two planets that meet at a mathematical angle within the structure of the zodiac belt which is 360 degrees in circumference. The energies that are created can be a help or a hindrance depending on the angle of the planets involved. For example, the Moon placed in Taurus is happy to be in this zodiac sign. However, the Moon might make a square (90 degree) aspect to Mars, creating emotional tension that would need some kind of release, since the Moon is passive in energy and Mars is aggressive in its pursuit, coupled with the square which is a tense aspect. On the other hand if the Moon made a trine (120 degree) aspect to Mars, the energy would be different, since the aspect is supportive, and in this case the Moon finds an outlet to express the more 'outward' tendencies of Mars. There are varying aspects but here I am going to concentrate on the major ones.

The Conjunction (0 degrees)

This happens when two or more planets are located in the same sign only a few degrees apart, the widest possible being 8 degrees from either side of each other. This is a powerful aspect where the two planets work closely with each other; it can be positive or negative depending on the planets involved, for instance Saturn and Mars would work against each other whereas the Sun and Jupiter would be positive in their approach. The conjunction accentuates the quality of the planets involved. When the outer planets form this major aspect with each other, it is a time of change and structural shifts on the world stage, depending which zodiac sign these planets are trying to work through. However, for the outer planets to make a conjunction is actually very rare, because they move so slowly through the zodiac. A Saturn and Uranus conjunction occurs every forty-six years, as an example. This means that when two outer planets do come together it can create some explosive results that make us humans re-evaluate our lives and futures. This is when astrology can begin to understand the cycles humankind must go through if we are to evolve spiritually.

The Opposition (180 degrees)

This is when the positions of two planets that are within the 360 degree zodiac circle are 180 degrees in opposition from each other. This is known as a hard aspect, because the zodiac signs that are involved are opposites in the zodiac belt.

Aries – Libra

Taurus – Scorpio

Gemini – Sagittarius

Cancer – Capricorn

Leo – Aquarius

Virgo – Pisces

Opposites in the zodiac have great and karmic lessons to learn from each other; however, their energies are different in temperament. So any planets that are travelling in opposite signs will create cross-purposes in their objectives, because a planet is a living consciousness. The push and pull of two planets at opposites can help to ignite and allow change to come even if it can be rather dramatic. The opposing forces of the meeting of two planets will bring in change but also turbulence and confusion at times. The orb of the aspect is again 8 degrees either side of the planets involved, although the nearer they are to each other in orbit the more powerful, for instance an 8 degree orb would be a weak aspect as opposed to 2 degrees which would be strong.

The Trine (120 degrees)

The Trine aspect is known as a soft aspect, because of the flowing energies of the zodiac signs that are involved which are in the same element.

Fire – Aries, Leo, Sagittarius

Air – Gemini, Libra, Aquarius

Earth – Taurus, Virgo, Capricorn

Water – Cancer, Scorpio, Pisces

When two planets meet at a 120 degree aspect, the two energies tend to create an easygoing time in terms of the signs that are part of the trine. For example, Venus could be placed in Aquarius and 120 degrees away it meets Saturn which is in Libra in the zodiac wheel. Again this can also cause some laziness within the trine aspect and indeed trouble can occur because of the planets involved, but generally it is a positive aspect.

The Square (90 degrees)

This aspect is a hard aspect that brings about a certain amount of repetitive and destructive tension, because the zodiac signs are in the same triplicities.

Cardinal – Aries, Cancer, Libra, Capricorn

Fixed – Taurus, Leo, Scorpio, Aquarius

Mutable – Gemini, Virgo, Sagittarius, Pisces

Tension is felt through the association of the triplicities because there is no 'instinct' to be able to break a pattern. An example is Jupiter in Scorpio that makes a 90 degree aspect to Mars in Aquarius; the fixed nature of these two signs can cause a stagnating situation and these energies need careful handling if they are going to live with these two planets in aspect. However, it is an aspect that you cannot ignore and plenty of lessons need to be learnt. Therefore something positive can come from a square aspect. The difficulty might be that the tensions experienced by the square could cause confrontation within the structure of the zodiac signs that are involved; again careful handling of these energies can also serve to break old patterns as.

The Sextile (60 degrees)

The Sextile is a very positive aspect because the signs that are involved are elements that combine to help each other. For example fire and air signs work well together, and earth and water do too; these elements in the zodiac wheel are no more than two signs away from each other. The implication of this is a 'nature' that can work well in getting things moving in the area or planets that are involved.

The Inconjunct (150 degrees)

This is an aspect that is seen by many as a weak aspect that does not have an impact. Personally, I disagree with this view. This aspect causes problems because the elements and signs that are involved to create this aspect have no relationship with each other. The planets have to be 150 degrees apart, and that means that there is little relationship with the two signs. An example might be Mars in Taurus making an inconjunct to Venus in Libra.

Taurus is an earth sign and Libra an air sign, which means that too much of these elements create dust. This aspect means that lessons need to be learnt because these internal conflicts will not go away. The inconjunct is an aspect that can cause confusion and unease which leads to restless and impulsive actions.

There are other minor aspects within the structure of a natal chart. However, within future chapters of this book I shall be using the aspects I have described since they relate to more outward symbolic messages for the world. The aspects can determine the cycles that we have to experience within the context of planet Earth, coupled with the signs that predominate at any moment in history or the future of these cosmic alignments. What is important is that we have an understanding that these transits (planets moving around the zodiac creating aspects) are not fixed but are constantly changing and moving forward into new positions in the sky. Therefore whatever 'hard' aspects that humanity has coming up are momentary energies designed to wake us up, or to fit another piece in the jigsaw. Aspects get things moving; they are creative in their endeavours and they adapt to circumstances. By looking at past aspects and the planets involved we can again begin to determine when major shifts and changes in the world took place and how humans responded to their energies.

Conjunctions with Planets

Jupiter – Saturn

This conjunction is always a period of change and more importantly new beginnings, because the expansive qualities of Jupiter are given structure through the vibrations of the planet Saturn. Jupiter is always trying to over-extend itself and tries to deliver more than it can. This means that a certain religious expectation can happen when these two planets meet in a conjunction. This aspect happens every twenty years, the last being in the year 2000 when the millennium fever of a new dawn and optimism gave way to disappointment as the West was shaken by the events of 9/11. Before 2000, the last conjunction between Jupiter and Saturn took place in 1980. We remember the rise of Thatcher from the instability of the 1970's in economic terms, and the marriage of Prince Charles and Princess Diana; the optimistic atmosphere was soon to be scorned with a yet more unstable job market in the years that followed and a period of overhaul. This is how this aspect between these two planets works; Jupiter inspires and gives us false hope while the planet Saturn makes us work hard for what we want. It is important that at these times we do use the energy of Jupiter to reinvigorate our consciousness so that we do become more optimistic in our approach, but at the same time that we do not allow our world ego to be at the mercy of Jupiter's rays, in other words we must remain upbeat but practical in our application. Saturn is the master of limitations and teaches our collective unconsciousness lessons that we must learn to develop.

Saturn – Uranus

The headmaster meets the great awakener – waves will be created or clouds may be generated. This aspect does seem to be affected more by the signs that these two planets meet in, as regards the outcome. However, there is a nice balance between the old and the new when these two planets meet in a conjunction, because with every structure a revaluation and development needs to take place. Therefore these two planets can have a powerful effect on the world. But again it depends on the signs that are involved. These two planets meet every forty-five years and can contribute to a structural change over a period of three years. There is another way that these two planets can react and that is through devastation, especially in the zodiac signs of Scorpio, Taurus and Leo, for these signs are fixed in nature and therefore hang on to the status quo leading to near lockdown before Uranus overpowers and changes the balance. The sign of Aquarius is the only fixed sign that I have not included because Saturn and Uranus both rule this sign; therefore they can achieve positive results, a revolution with planning.

Saturn – Neptune

Saturn likes to know where it stands and how to maintain the old, while Neptune likes to confuse Saturn with esoteric messages that Saturn cannot possibly understand, at least initially. When these two meet is seems an unlikely combination, yet limitations and spirituality can work hand in hand as long as they respect each other. Saturn has powerful vibrations and tends to not want interference from other planets. However, Neptune has a funny ability to get underneath the skin of Saturn. Spirituality in general is given the ability to be worked into the more conservative (Saturn) values of society. But this can also mean that a certain fanatical approach to religion can manifest. Both these planets are opposing energies in essence, and can be difficult to work with since Saturn likes rules and Neptune hates boundaries. The lesson for these two (in a conjunction) is to work together to bring a higher state of consciousness (Neptune) through the work and ambition of the world (Saturn tenth house ruler).

Saturn – Pluto

Here we have two planets that have such heavyweight energy to them it would be naïve to expect boundless positivity; these two can literally tear out each other's hearts. Power is the word that encapsulates the meeting between these two planets, for each wants to control and discipline the other. Therefore in simple terms we have a power struggle that can only end in destruction, which can nevertheless help to heal the past and bring in a new dawn. There is no grey area with these two, because the energy is too grounded in rays to not do anything. When these two meet wars can literally break out, for example (one point in history when Saturn and Pluto came together) the beginning of the First World War in 1914. However, Pluto wants us to clear out the old to make way for the new, as Saturn helps to begin the journey of stabilising the future. Sweeping changes and a need to shake the foundations (Pluto, Hades) are all themes here as the world is on a rollercoaster on the 'Dark side of the Moon'.

Uranus – Pluto

A conjunction which brings major changes that end in violence and are explosive in how they are expressed; these two planets have the 'fixed' element (they rule Aquarius and Scorpio). Revolution is in the air and the might of these two planets can have an unbalancing effect, changing society for good. Uranus always wants to break old structures, and Pluto is always looking for the motivations that lie beneath the surface. It is a period of profound readjustment where the implications are great. Since Uranus rules lightning, the thunderbolt that comes can surprise everyone, most importantly the authorities. No stone is left unturned with these two planets in conjunction. They are going to be causing most of the issues over the next eight years, and the first test of this is going to be from the period of June 2012 to September 2012, especially in the UK's chart where it will hit sensitive points; remember Uranus is in Aries and Pluto is in Capricorn.

Uranus – Neptune

These two planets combine in an artistic way creating new forms of enlightenment that can have a profound effect on humanity. On the other side of things it can also cause confusion because the two energies are high in ideals, meaning that there is no grounding between the two. This can have devastating problems if not channelled correctly and can lead to corruption and falseness. One of the best ways to utilise this energy is to redefine the boundaries that were set previously, and to make them much more adaptable to the new way of being and thinking. These two (at the time of writing this book) just recently helped to raise the consciousness to a higher vibration. Another aspect to this conjunction is the increase and development of scientific research; the findings will depend on the zodiac sign where these two meet, the recent journey of these two planets in Aquarius and Pisces in mutual reception is indicative of the 'new world order and genetic engineering' that we are now experiencing.

Neptune – Pluto

This is a powerhouse combination that produces the more mystical aspects of humanity, but also scandal and disgrace with public figures, which can last twenty years, because these are two slow-moving planets. The sexuality of these meeting in aspect can also create a highly-charged atmosphere and also a possessive reference to sex that holds almost religious connota-tions. The allure of illusion and power is great with these two planets and needs to be controlled, because unseen powers can be greater than any material.

The above combinations of planets coming together gives a general insight into the inner workings of when two energies come together and what they can transmit to Earth. These powerful outer planets have a more generational input and are therefore extremely important as regards where they are and what aspects they make to each other. Conjunctions are an extreme energy that are at the centre of two planets involved in the same sign. From these cycles we can begin to deduce what could happen when these cycles meet again.

Chapter 9

'The Drugs Don't Work'
Richard Ashcroft, 1997

One of the major themes over the last forty years in relation to
the planets' cycles and their impact on humans, and how we
interact, is the rise in mental illness. Increased knowledge can
create an overwhelming burden on the mental faculties, and this
can lead to confusion and the inability to function within
society's structure. Here we must look at two planets in the
context of how they relate to the rise in mental illness. Mercury
and Uranus are the rulers of the mind, Mercury the lower
(meaning everyday uses, ie writing, speaking, learning) while
Uranus is the higher (discoveries, invention, clairvoyance).
Mercury works quickly as an energy and because it is an inner
planet the aspects that it makes to other planets are more
personal. However, Uranus is different because it is seen in
astrology as a more generational planet; this is due to its orbit,
every seven years changing to another zodiac sign. If Uranus
aspects one of the other outer planets then we have a shift in our
mental perception that can cause unusual thoughts and disturbances. One of the major predictions over the period 2012–2020
is an increase in mental illness; this is due to what has already
been stated many times in this book: higher consciousness.
Uranus is a planet that works happily in that higher vibration,
but as individuals are we ready to embrace the higher states of
reality? Society within the western world in the last forty years
has been built around and organised in terms of the mental
layers of our consciousness, more than the spiritual, emotional
and in some ways the physical, although the last has been
pushed forward more by the increase in sports, and health and

fitness. If we think of television, advertising, technology more than anything else, these things have a direct effect on the mind, because the mind is what is used most in participating in these activities. All of these activities are ruled by Uranus apart from advertising (which has a Neptunian concept), but the vehicle that displays the advertising, for example television, is Uranus.

Within the period 2012–2020, Uranus goes through two zodiac signs, the first being Aries from 2011–2018. This combination is going to create the most serious problems in terms of mental perception and confusion. The vibration of Aries (that rules the head) will not only cause impulsive behaviour but also an over-stimulus of ideas, in particular those that are trying to break old traditions of how the masculine gender acts within society. Aries is the first point of the zodiac; it starts as we enter the spring equinox and therefore relates to the youth section of society. Here we have a major upheaval in how the youth fit into the modes of expression that have been implemented by the adult generation. However, the other major shift is the increase in mental illness within youth culture that could put strain on governments and result in a breakdown of moral guidance in terms of finding solutions to the problem. Uranus works mentally (air) in a higher level to Mercury; it is the planet of flashes of inspiration and perception. That perception radiates within the eastern philosophy of the third eye chakra. The opening of this point between the temples of the brow, as a general shift in human consciousness, can help us to become more at one with universal thinking and telepathic thoughts by using higher states within the mind. But if the mind is only partially developed because of the age of the recipient of this higher knowledge (Uranus) then the mind becomes clouded and unsure, causing mental distraction and a split in the thinking process. Another issue that causes mental confusion is the experimentation of substances (legal or illegal) which all come under the rulership of the planet

Neptune. During the period 2012–2020 Neptune is travelling in the zodiac sign of Pisces which is its natural home. Just because the sign of Pisces and the planet Neptune go together hand in glove, it does not mean that all is positive. During this period there will be an increased need to be spiritually uplifted and new forms of religion will be born. The other area that becomes intensified is artistic pursuits and creativity, for the need to express what is around us through channelled (Neptune) thoughts and other worldly vibrations (from different dimensions that are constantly around us) will grow. This need to 'go beyond' the material world and transcend the ordinary will lead to an increase in the use of substances to achieve these aims in a quicker time. This has already been occurring over the last fifty years at a rapid pace (as with many cultures historically) but it is the environment and mental state of the participants that should be considered. The combination of Uranus and Neptune can be very spiritually rewarding. But what must be looked at is the 'shadow' aspect of each zodiac sign, ie Aries and Pisces to gain an understanding of the complexities that will arise for the planets travelling through these signs.

We have one sign at the start of the zodiac cycle and one at the end, meaning that the energy between the Pisces ending and the Aries beginning needs to be properly understood. Aries is always trying to get away from the 'darker' elements of itself; it wants to focus more on the 'day force' rather than the 'night force' (as stated by the late American astrologer Dane Rudhyar). It is therefore important that Aries is free to express its individuality through direct experience. Pisces on the other hand wishes to experience the more mystical states of life as the higher self obtains knowledge through these rays. The importance of beginning and ending is absorbing within the current climate of planetary set-ups, but it also signifies a shift in world view and social change. The planets Uranus (ruler of Aquarius, the higher mind) and Neptune (ruler of Pisces, the higher self) will help us all to reach new levels of understanding and the completion of a cycle, which is stated by the age of Aquarius.

The younger generation and indeed those who were born in the last twenty years will feel isolated from the governmentrun society, and will therefore wish to escape from it (Neptune). Drugs have always been around and will be much more widely used by the general population during the next ten years. This is because humans will begin to feel more restricted by society and will have no way of rebelling (Uranus) against it, so seeking escapism through drugs (Neptune in Pisces). The positive affirmation from these two planets (within these two signs) is a rise in the level of humanitarian (Uranus) awareness (Neptune). But if society has not learnt the lessons from the past (which does seem to be the case), then more people will feel a need for escape. This does beg the question: is mental illness created by society rather than genetic factors?

I believe that the way we have responded to the planets' vibrations and pulls in the past has contributed to a breakdown in the human link with the six senses and is continuing to create mental disturbances and conflict within personalities. The period –2012–2020 will mark the crisis point in how we deal with these cases, and the only way to change this downfall is to change the way society is built. The planets are energies that 'want' the Earth to have similar vibrations, so that the other planets (being living bodies) can interact to balance the universe. However, it is how we humans interpret these rays that determines the outcome. To put it in more simple terms, our planet is currently out of sync with the natural flow of energies, and before we can move forward we must realign ourselves, which means getting rid of the clutter and having a total revaluation of society and how we live our lives. Uranus in Aries will bring about change, because

Aries is a fire sign and cardinal. In other words it does not simply sit back and wait, it creates change. Pisces in Neptune is much more passive in energy and will be less clear in its processes, leading to murmurs and tremors in its expression; it will focus on the 'night force' of our natures, while Uranus in Aries will work through the 'day force'. This is because the two signs meet at the spring equinox on the 20th of March, when the cycle of winter ends and spring begins. There is a complex relationship between the two signs; when working in harmony they bring great renewal, but if their cycle is disturbed in any way then the rhythm breaks down. The semi-sextile aspect between these two planets will help to neutralise their most negative effects, yet it is up to us to respond positively to these energies.

The predictions for these two planets in the signs over the period 2012–2020 are an increase in mental illness in young people coupled with new spiritual and social innovations. For example in 1848 (the last time Neptune travelled in Pisces) we saw the rise of the Spiritualist Movement, and Karl Marx produced his 'Communist Manifesto'. In 1849 we saw the launch of the Pre-Raphaelite artistic Movement. Uranus in Aries will tear down the structures and roles of the gender of man, similar to when Uranus was in Libra's opposite sign of Aries, a time in the early seventies when the Feminist Movement really started to take form and gain ground culturally. Aries will focus its energy on the word 'masculine' and new roles will start to be implemented; the male gender will have to 'grow up' in the sense of their own spirituality within the framework of their gender.

Genetic engineering will also increase, causing much anxiety about the 'perfect human'. The cost will be huge, because the boundaries (Neptune) will not be clear and so moral standards will need to be stated. This will be a period when we will see aspects of genetic engineering become near disasters, making us question its use for the future. An increase in diseases connected to the brain will be seen at this period, having reactions on the nervous system (Uranus in Aries) especially in combination with the fixed stars of Sheat, Difda and Algenib. These are placed in the early degrees of Aries (30 degrees in a sign). This means that the early stages of Uranus moving into Aries are going to be the most difficult, ie from 2011–2014. This is a period when revolution is in the air and violence will be seen as the way to get the authorities to listen. However, with Neptune passing through Pisces, governments may be deluded in their thinking, unable to listen to the public and their opinions. So we are all in for a tough time, and the question arises: what planet over the next eight years will bring stability and focus?

Chapter 10

Saturn's Future

During the next eight years the planet Saturn and its cycle will shed light on those areas that need to be limited and given responsibility before reaching achievement. The sign which Saturn occupies for two and a half years will determine which areas of our human consciousness need to be restructured. Without Saturn as our guiding force we would be at the mercy of other planets' schemes but with no follow-through; that is the greatness of Saturn, you work hard with it, you get the results! In this chapter I will show how Saturn's cycles will have a direct bearing on how we come out of this crisis point. Saturn is a planet that can bring stability to a country or individual if allowed, meaning that Saturn can put limitations on itself, because the rays of the planet have to be directed with focus and determination. The zodiac sign that Saturn travels through will shed light on the energies that Saturn has to respond to. The fire signs (Aries, Leo and Sagittarius) find Saturn's energy overbearing and too restrictive for their spontaneous natures, although during a transit of Saturn the fire signs can (when used wisely) accomplish much in that period when Saturn is committing its energy to the element of fire. The air signs can respond well to Saturn, especially Aquarius and Libra, because Saturn is the old ruler of Aquarius and Saturn is exalted in Libra. The sign Gemini also receives discipline from Saturn through the mind (Mercury). The earth signs can go one way or another; Capricorn is ruled by Saturn, this allows Saturn to really blossom. Taurus and Virgo, however, can become stuck under the influence of Saturn, or can become ruthless. The water signs find Saturn too restrictive in energies, because water signs like to explore emotions and not feel the weight of expectation on a material level (the waySaturn likes to guide us). Saturn needs time to 'bed in' its ideas and energies; it is a planet that works slowly to achieve its aims, but can be devoid of human emotion, preferring the arena of tangible results to abstract thoughts.

Saturn in Libra

January 2012 – September 2012

The word that is associated with Saturn in Libra is 'balance'. In fact Saturn is exalted in Libra and is therefore comfortable in this placement. However, diplomacy is the key to finding success with Saturn travelling in Libra. This is to do with the political arena and how we get along with allies and enemies. During this period there is the ability to create a more communicative (air) exchange of ideas that can suit many different countries, especially in the realm of war and revolution. The Middle East has certain astrological aspects that will bring it to the forefront during this period of instability. Saturn wants to enable the leaders of countries to talk and act (cardinal). However, the UK (which has a Libran ascendant) will be deeply affected at this time by its own image in the world, leading to chaos in the later stages of 2012 in its political system and affecting the Prime Minister. The US' chart will be under Saturn's rays in the eleventh house, making high ideals a thing of the past at this period. In other words, an almost 'back to basics' approach will become the norm, especially with the economic situation. The trine aspect between Jupiter and Saturn services a certain amount of healing and optimism with the western world, but just when we think we have stability Saturn enters Scorpio (ruled by Pluto the planet of transformation and rebirths).

Saturn in Scorpio

November 2012 – September 2015

This is a period that could test us all and bring about devastating destruction of governmental orders and capitalist gains. Like the Phoenix rising from the ashes, the first thing that needs to happen is for a metaphorical death to occur. Pluto, Scorpio's ruler, is in the zodiac sign of Capricorn which rules the establishment. Pluto and Saturn are focusing on the undercurrents of society and bringing into focus those parts that we as humans would rather forget. So there is an element of Saturn in Scorpio that will play havoc with our 'fears' in a society that seems at this stage to be at breaking point. But there is a purpose to this ordeal, for Saturn in Scorpio is reminding us that the structures we have put in place in the past, do not work any longer. The result from this experience is that we will all feel the need to change how we live our lives; there will be an unrelenting need for us all to have some deeper meaning to our existence. This 'shudder' in our collective unconsciousness will be felt for years to come, for Scorpio is fixed in purpose and wants to create firm new foundations that can be used for future generations. The results are extreme because the temperament of the sign Scorpio (the symbolism) conveys a nature that has a sting in its tail, but on a deeper level its ability to transform old patterns is formidable. During this period we can expect great changes in the way we view life as a whole, for remember Scorpio is a water sign and this denotes emotional empathy and understanding. On an individual level the need to 'connect' with others will be high, and relationships will need to be more fulfilling and have lasting impressions. The other aspect of Saturn in Scorpio is found in hidden mysteries and occult learning, so new ways of experiencing other dimensions and an increase of our knowledge of quantum physics will occur at this time. Saturn is all about gaining and increasing the intellectual thought process. Parts of society where the government has a greater say will come under scrutiny, particularly the prison system and how we treat criminals in society. This is a period that will see new forms of rehabilitation for people who stand outside society out of choice or circumstance. However, these 'new forms' may not be the answer, because they will focus on restriction (Saturn) and manipulation (Scorpio) to gain results.

Saturn in Sagittarius

October 2015 – December 2017

The heaviness of Saturn passing through Scorpio is now relieved as Saturn begins its journey into Sagittarius. The more philosophical side of our existence comes into play and with good reason after the shift of Scorpio. Countries will be seeking help from each other; during Saturn in Scorpio a major war will occur involving the US and the UK, and as these countries become strained in their policies and opinions, the basic theme is that we are still not out of the woods yet. Saturn and Sagittarius don't have a great relationship with each other when they first meet; they must learn to respect each other before they can make progress but once they do great things can happen. Sagittarius is fire and mutable – it likes to flex its intellectual muscles and to have many ideas and constant stimulation. Saturn on the other hand is cautious in its approach and wants to make sure there is a safety net before it embarks on anything new. So lessons have to be learnt, and education will be one aspect that will be changed and revised, ie how we educate our children and our approach to learning in general. The US will be the hardest hit under Saturn's influence since it will transit the first house, meaning a new more mature identity will develop during this time. This is where Saturn can come into its own, making sure that all those Sagittarian ideas have some kind of focus that can be used to benefit society as a whole. Higher education will be overhauled in the West, making it easier to gain higher qualifications with a new degree system. However, during this period Saturn will square Neptune in Pisces, helping to fuel the possibility that if we are not careful then we could be trying to chase a utopian dream that does not become a reality. The tension between these two planets is immense since they are opposites in energy and temperament. They can learn a lot from each other, but they can also send confusing messages that make it almost impossible to communicate on the same wavelength. The strongest period of this aspect is in the summer of 2016 when the square will be exact; this time will create havoc in terms of finances and anything to do with oil and gas. The environment will be addressed at this time making an issue in relation to trade with foods from other countries and a shortage in agricultural back-up. 2016 will be a year when we will all realise the consequences of our past actions and how they will or will not shape our future. The dynamic energy at this point will change things for the next thirty years. Sagittarius is optimistic by nature because of its ruling planet Jupiter, and this could be our saviour; religious morals could overtake logic and the battles of opinions in that area will cause upheaval.

Saturn in Capricorn

January 2018 – December 2020

Saturn now resides in its natural home of Capricorn, meaning that this planet is at its most powerful in terms of the energetic shifts that it creates. The world by now will need the implementation of new structures and rules, so that future generations will be able to learn from the past. During Saturn's transit in Capricorn our collective survival techniques and ambitions will start to become much more apparent, and new leaders will come into powerful positions at this time in the West. The UK will be revived under this transit, and new opportunities for growth will occur, especially in the economic markets. However, the business world will shift its priorities and the environmental market (Capricorn, earth sign) will be the place where new jobs and careers will develop. The US will also find that this period will bring stability in terms of its economy since Saturn will be travelling in the second house of building for the future. The serious overtones of Saturn will be felt by everyone as a realisation dawns of the universal need to function at a community level and less so from an individual standpoint. Any planet that enters the sign of Capricorn is nearing the end of a cycle; the signs Aquarius and Pisces are the last stages, it is therefore vital that we as 'beings' are listening to the needs of the universe. In seasonal terms the zodiac sign of Capricorn is a time when we have to fend for ourselves and become ready for the winter months. What also must be considered at this time is that Pluto is travelling through the sign of Capricorn. The period January 2020 to February 2020 will see massive shake-ups and bold decisions being made because of the conjunction between Saturn and Pluto at this point. This is another 'crisis point'. One reason for this is that if we look back at past history we can deduce the energy that these two planets create when they meet. In 1946–1948 Saturn and Pluto were travelling in Leo, and this marked the start of the 'Cold War'. Assassinations and power struggles tend to occur at this period, an there is also a non-emotional approach to the world that can lead to significant survival instincts but sometimes a lack of humanity. The monarchy in the UK could also come under pressure at this time, leading it to hold on to values that no longer serve their purpose. Scandal will occur with a male in the Royal Family that will lead to them revaluating how they conduct themselves and how they fit in with society and their image. 2020 is not an easy year for humanity as Saturn and Pluto are planets that are not soft in their approach or easy to work with, unless you are prepared to seek fulfilment by using a 'no frills' attitude. However, as we come to the end of 2020,

Saturn travels into the sign of Aquarius bringing a more human-itarian outlook and a need to be more equal in dealings with the general public in relation to attitudes and political th-emes. The planets at this point also indicate governmental change in relation to political parties and a new way of dealing with government in the UK.

This is a period where Charles Darwin's theme 'Survival of the fittest' could be employed by all. If we get through this period then we can start to seriously build for the future and beyond with renewed spiritual and structural outlooks.

Chapter 11

How to Survive 2012–2020 Through Each Sun Sign

This next chapter focuses on how each Sun sign will respond to the planetary changes over this eight-year period. If you are aware of your rising sign, then please read the description of that sign, because that will also indicate how you will deal with the energies that will be affecting certain sections of your life and path. Sun sign astrology is one aspect of astrology; however, the Sun sign is basically our vitality and how we see ourselves in the great scheme of things. Remember Sun sign astrology is based fundamentally on the seasons more than the constellations, therefore when a planet enters or aspects a sign, the natural rhythm of that sign is displaced, changed or pulled in another direction. Some signs will benefit more than others, in other words some signs will make great leaps and bounds during this fraught eight years. History informs us that 'change' is the one thing that is certain in life and that each of us is responsible for how history will look upon and teach us in years to come. The idea of a collective unity is not a new one, and the power of people coming together during difficult times can help everyone to raise their vibration energies for a higher cause and use the planets' rays to overcome trials and tribulations as well as to find positive renewal. By looking at your own Sun sign you can determine which areas between the years 2012–2020 you need to be aware of on a personal level.

Aries

This is one sign that will be affected deeply during this period, contributing to a shift in consciousness with all individuals born under this Sun sign. The coming eight years will see Arians becoming the leaders in their fields and also the rebels, making some of them the outcasts of society. The reason for this is the influence of the planet Uranus that is transiting in the sign of Aries through to May 2018. The main theme for Arians is 'change' and to not resist the opportunities that will present themselves, no matter how unconventional they appear. Aries is a fire sign and cardinal, you like to push yourself forward and to feel that life is taking you somewhere, no matter where that is. Uranus is a planet that likes to bring disruption to any sign that it occupies. It is important that you realise that nothing is going remain stagnated at this junction. Aries can become incredibly restless under the influence of Uranus, making it hard for Arians to feel grounded in their abilities. During the period January 2012 to October 2012, Saturn is still travelling in the sign of Libra, your opposite sign; over the last couple of years you might have felt that whatever you did was not appreciated by the people around you, as if they were putting a dampener on your plans. In October Saturn will travel into the sign of Scorpio, making an impact on your solar eighth house. This is the house which rules people's money and any business ventures that are entered into at this time should be carefully examined. Aries is a sign that tends to be self-employed or at least have a business partner. This is because Arians are natural leaders, and need space to express their individuality. Uranus coupled with Saturn in Scorpio will contribute to a time when rash decisions may be taken; there is a need for danger (Scorpio eighth house) that dominates your personality. How you deal with this energy is up to you, but the 'need' to psychologically chase the more absurd ideas could push you and the people around you in many directions, and this is especially true in the period 2013–2015. The lesson during this time is to make sure that you look at all of the options that are available to you; patience is a word that is not attached to you a great deal, because of your ruling planet Mars.

Uranus (by being in the zodiac sign of Aries) is at the start of a new eighty-four-year cycle. Aries is about conquering new lands metaphorically, so that we can enter a new period of change and excitement, and all these descriptions are part of the jigsaw puzzle of how the sign Aries needs to approach this eight-year period. Jupiter is another planet that can contribute to internal and external changes that profoundly affect how a sign copes and gains wisdom. From June 2012 to June 2013 the planet Jupiter is in the zodiac sign of Gemini. Aries' third house is ignited by Jupiter as knowledge and communications will be expanded; there may also be unfocused energy that flitters away on wild dreams (Uranus/Jupiter). Arians will again need to be careful, as plans will be ambitious, and the far-sighted visions will help many people in the long term. In June 2013 Jupiter changes signs again travelling into the sign of Cancer, marking a point in Arians' lives when the home environment becomes key. The transition will be heavy due to the opposition on the angles of the IC (internal) and the MC (external) to the planet Pluto in Capricorn. The need to shift values and pressures from family will force you to take responsibilities much more seriously. The Uranus influence could also make an impact as it wants you to break away from old patterns, but the fourth house is all about tradition in structure. However, Jupiter is a beneficial planet that expands awareness and sets the motions of movement and creative flair. The real magic in Arians' lives is the period July 2014–2015 when Jupiter is transiting the fifth house of joy, pleasure and creativity in the house of Leo. Because of the fire placement of Jupiter the Sun (Aries) is now able to express itself in its full capacity. This is a period of vigour and freedom for many Arians, and for the year 2015 the planet Saturn will be in the sign of Sagittarius making a grand trine aspect in the fire element. Arians should use this energy to get projects and ideas off the ground but also to develop their own spirituality and purpose. The fire energy burns bright for Sun and ascendant

Arians and should be taken as a green light to move forward in all aspects of their daily life. In August 2015, Jupiter enters the sign of Virgo situated in the sixth house, when work plans will need attention to detail. Jupiter as an energy does bring about a certain growth in whatever area it touches. The sixth house rules work, health and service matters; it also helps Arians to look at their lifestyle and how they balance work and domestic matters. However, in September 2016 Jupiter moves into Libra in the house of partnerships. For many Arians this could prove to be a critical period as any relationship that you are now involved in could be under strain, because of your need to break away from old patterns. Remember at some point (depending on what date you were born in the period of Aries) Jupiter will come into opposition with Uranus creating feelings of restlessness and idealism in the area of relationships and how a partner sees you. This period will be not be fully realised until Jupiter enters Scorpio in October 2017 when the expansion of your consciousness (perception) will have consequences on your actions, for Arians at this time will be required to explain their new beliefs and re-examine them. Then in December 2017 Saturn will move into its own sign of Capricorn entering your tenth house of worldly ambitions. This will set a new cycle for Aries who will now be at the forefront of shaping the new structures (Saturn) in terms of business and institutions (Neptune twelfth house).

In May 2018 the planet Uranus leaves its passage through Aries to go into the sign of Taurus meaning that Aries can now begin to settle. The last seven years have been dominated with the 'need' to tear down the old traditions of what it means to be an Aries in the twenty-first century, so from 2018 the building process begins in earnest for Aries.

Taurus

Change does not come easy for the bull; Taurus is a fixed earth sign and would rather remain in its comfort zone where it knows what is coming up next in life or at least what to expect. But like all of the signs, Taurus needs to grow and develop. More than any other sign in the zodiac the Taurus in the last ten years is the sign that has dominated in the following: psychics, healers, clairvoyants and alternative health practitioners. There are deeper reasons for this change in the Taurus emotional make-up that have esoteric implications. Taurus is known as a materialistic zodiac sign. The basis of this assumption is that Taurus likes its 'security' and that society's perception of achieving this is through money, or in other words it is the acquisition of goods through hard work. This has certainly been the case in the past, but all of the signs cannot remain static, because like everything, even astrology, it is evolving. The word that is closely associated with Taurus is 'growth' and the need to build for the future. Within the period 2012–2020 the emphasis is growth for all of the signs and over the last ten years the sign Taurus has needed to learn to let go of the promise of material gain equalling security. This has manifested in a lot of soul-searching for the Taurus which has meant a more spiritual existence and a shift taking place. The point is that by taking a more spiritual view of life and direction the Taurus can help to rebuild society in a way that will concentrate on more simple and energetic principles. Uranus which is the great awakener of the planets is travelling through the sign of Aries in the Taurus twelfth solar house, the house of endings and karma. This is important because the 'shift' in Taurus is actually more of an unconsciousness, they are not that aware of the big undercurrents that are shifting and challenging their firm beliefs. Uranus directs its rebellious energy by creating the feeling that a storm is brewing, you can sense it in the air as the rumblings of thunder can be heard in the distance. Taurus will be feeling the same, as the shift is coming over the next six years and the thunder is getting closer. As it approaches the first house, lightning will strike. Taureans will need to learn to trust their internal instincts and their ability to sense (earth) when things are changing and to go with the flow when they do. The planets Jupiter and Saturn are good indicators of how Taurus will respond to the challenges on an individual as well as a global scale. Jupiter in 2012 is placed in the sign of Gemini which for Taurus rules the second house of possessions and self-esteem and how we see you in terms of status. Jupiter is a planet that brings a wealth of luck and expansive thinking. This need to look beyond the usual methods of making money is an important step in your own inner development and for Taurus generally it heralds spiritual growth in the materialistic world. In October 2012 Saturn (the planet of limitations) goes into the sign of your opposite, Scorpio. This is in the house of partnerships ruled by Pluto (the planet of the underworld). Feelings that have been put metaphorically into a box will begin to manifest in partners or those close to you, so that a mirror of your more shadowy aspects starts to develop. This is a time over the next two and a half years when your views about the sharing aspect in life will be tested to the full. The second house and the seventh are fundamentally in combat with each other. The second house is about an individual approach directed by Jupiter in the Venus house and the seventh house is about sharing; the inconjuct 150 degrees apart in aspect always creates inner tensions that have to be resolved and balanced. In June 2013 Jupiter revives the need for Taureans to communicate their feelings finally as the planet enters the sign of Cancer. Home becomes the key factor because of Cancer, but the third house has an educational twist as the need to express ideas and keep busy contradicts the Taurus' slowness of pace that is naturally part of their emotional make-up. However, this is a period that sees the Taurus reacting emotionally to world events in a much more direct way. This leads us back to Uranus in the twelfth house. Taurus is starting to tap into other energies that are not tangible and therefore, for a sign that is so reliant on the senses, it is going through a major transformation. But it is not until December 2014 that we start to see these undercurrents become much more apparent as Saturn enters Sagittarius in the Taurus ninth house. The ninth house is the place of ideals that are greater than the third house since it deals with more abstract thoughts and perceptions. Saturn is a conformer that builds rather than destroys; insights and intuitions are within the conscious reach and are readily available to vocalise (Taurus) opinions that are not yet recognised. Think of Karl Marx, Bono, Sigmund Freud and Tony Blair, pesonalities all born under the Sun sign of Taurus who have had firm convictions and visionary ideas. The idea of spirituality becomes the benchmark for the sign of Taurus as they learn the process of the need to build new empires and to think with new concepts. In 2018 the planet Uranus enters Taurus as the lightning finally strikes and the thunder rips through the skies, a truly breath-taking moment. Coupled with Pluto passing through another earth sign (Capricorn), 2018 is a marked point astrologically. This is when the rebuilding process begins, meaning the new structure of society, second and tenth houses emphasised. Taurus will only survive, and by that I mean feel in control of their lives, during this difficult period, if they let go of their more material-istic values and concentrate on the more spiritual insights that they have been slowly acquiring.

Gemini

Gemini is a mutable air sign that uses its intellectual powers to survive in the world – communication is the food of the Gemini. Society in the West and now in the East is overpowered by technology and the need to communicate in a variety of different forms. Therefore you would think that the zodiac sign of Gemini would be in its element, and that especially in the period June 2012 to July 2013 this might be the case, as Jupiter is travelling in this sign. But the indicators on an esoteric level are a nervousness that seems to be greater than the ability to just 'be'. The twins are in a precarious position because the more choice there is, the more unstable Geminis become. Out of the entire zodiac signs the Gemini is the most youthful; it remains childlike in appearance and mental understanding. Like children who are over-stimulated, Geminis become tense, upset and unable to understand what they want, and that mental energy burns a hole in their spiritual and emotional layers. A Gemini is the eternal butterfly of the zodiac; it is at a loss as to which direction in should be following and so it begins to rely on the symbolism of trying to find its saviour, its twin soul-mate. The true meaning of the twins, the symbol of Gemini, is to unite the dual aspects of the Gemini personality (the mental and emotional) and to accept these differences and teach others the importance of knowledge of the 'inner you'. The Gemini might find the next eight years hard because they will have to create some union within themselves in order to combat that nervous quality that can sometimes haunt them. However, this is when the creative process can help them to rethink ideas and change viewpoints that can put them at an advantage. Children are most resilient to change and development and it is with this ethos that the Gemini can become happier; it is not external mental stimulation but internal spiritual insight. The grounding element of their development becomes important in realising during this period how they fit into the new waves of change that are about to occur in the structure of how we live our lives. The Gemini can become a beacon of hope and optimism during this crisis point if the he/she learns the art of balance. In October 2015 Saturn enters the opposite sign to Gemini which is Sagittarius; this axis will spark a renewal in self-discovery but also insecurities that will need to be controlled in order for the Gemini to grow. This is the point when Geminis can begin to bring structure to their mind and emotions, for if nothing else Saturn brings discipline. For the Gemini to feel comfortable in its environment the important feature is less focus on the mind and the thinking processes and more reliance on the higher self, the intuitive self. Meditation is highly beneficial for this zodiac sign.

Cancer

The Moon rules the sign of Cancer; it is feminine in principle and as a collective. The Moon's vibrations fluctuate in nature and energy and cause the Cancerian to at times feel emotionally exposed when vulnerable. That is why the Cancer is so much consumed by the home, because it is their one place of safety and protection from their moods and fears. In these challenging times, the zodiac sign of Cancer will have to be more ambitious in its approach to the outside world. Because the Moon's energies are nurturing, the Cancer individual needs to feel that they are making an impact on the world and using their skills to help humanity. It is perhaps worth noting that Cancer is a water element ruled by its emotions and is cardinal in quality, meaning that they need to feel they are moving forward in life. The period from 2012 to 2020 is crucial for the development of all of the signs and the zodiac sign of Cancer is no exception. From 2018 to 2020 Saturn makes its entry into Cancer's opposite sign of Capricorn. This will mark a time of stresses and strains for the Cancer individual who will feel that they are limited in their expression. However, this could also reveal a time of great healing and success if also a little hard work. Oppositions as an aspect always have a tense energy about them – it gets things moving. The Cancer needs to respond during these times with gusto and not to be fazed by anxiety or worries, things the Cancer tends to concentrate on. Cancer is placed as a sign in society as a meeting point between the active and the passive; the season is heralded by the summer solstice, a period when we have the longest day force. This gives us an indicator of the energy of the Cancer particularly in times of crisis. Cancer is the sign that helps humanity to find the knowledge of what is important in terms of the home, family and community, and it uses its energies to strive to build that base again in the new world. The Cancerian has a great survival instinct and anyone who is born with Cancer rising, Sun or Moon will have this inbuilt need to protect those close to them, for without this urge, morals begin to wane. From July 2013 to July 2014 the planet of expansion, Jupiter, travels into the sign of Cancer. This is the period when the need to break old patterns from the past and to become much more outgoing in opinions and indeed in lifestyle comes to the forefront. The Cancer individual will need to make great steps forward during this time if he/she is to keep up with the rest of the changes that the world is experiencing. The shifting boundaries that are being manipulated at this point will focus on individuals as they need to find some inner security (Cancer) that will make them stronger and able to deal with changing circumstances more readily. Cancer is one sign that needs to feel in control and therefore will feel at this point that they are left to their own devices, isolated from the rest of society. This is an illusion based on old emotional patterns that will need to be acknowledged in order for growth to begin.

Leo

Leaders and people in authority are there to break traditions and create new ideas and to have an ethos that will set the mark for future generations. The royal sign of Leo, fixed in temperament and fire in element, already has these characteristics embedded in its personality. The US President, Barack Obama (Leo Sun, Aquarius rising), perhaps shows these skills to great effect as a leader who is willing and able to change the dynamics of society even if that takes some time. The Leo individual is at the forefront of these changes because the Sun is the ruler of this sign and represents our vitality and growth within our creativity, ie without the Sun we are nothing. The survival instinct of the Leo is to 'create' and to be able to bring strength and purpose to the structure of society. The opposite sign of Leo is Aquarius and it is within this sign that we can find the true identity of the Leo. Aquarius is the sign of lost and ancient knowledge that we as humanity must accept and rediscover in order for us to maintain and develop as human beings on planet Earth. However, the Aquarius needs the Leo to 'action' (act out) these ideas, to put them into practice; so the axis between these two is intense because of the fixed quality and nature of these two signs. Leo must begin over the next eight years to recognise the information that is being displayed by the universe so that it can begin to 'teach' the masses. Leo is to be released or at least must obtain the feeling of lightness; again the opposite sign of Aquarius has been dominated over the last decade by the planets Uranus, Neptune and to a certain extent Chiron causing Leos to question their own identity. This has led to an awful lot of Leos feeling under-confident in relation to their abilities and the way that others perceive them. However, there will be a contrast over the next eight years that will make the sign of Leo much more positive in its approach and more in keeping with its natural skills. In a time of conflict between the wants of the general public and the ideas of governmental institutions, Leo individuals will become more prominent in their attempts to convey the feelings of other signs. This means that the natural leader role becomes more apparent for the Leo and this in turn creates a support system for the other eleven signs, because ultimately we rely on the Leo's creativity. This means that other signs are able to express themselves more freely; that is how astrology works as a collective within the zodiac signs. In July 2014 the fire planet Jupiter enters the sign of Leo, instigating a reawakening for many who are born under this sign. This is significant in the development of the Leo in the context of the planetary aspects. The push and pull of Pluto and Saturn will make it difficult for all to stand up and be counted, because many will feel ill at ease at the direction of the western world. But for Leos this could mark them out as people who are going to speak out against principles and authorities that make no sense. The quest for Leo is almost like the quest for the Holy Grail, but elusiveness is part of the charm of the Leo; it needs a quest and is quite happy to accept a more involved part of humanity's development, something that has been missing in the last few years.

Virgo

From the Leo's vitality we come to the Virgo's analytical nature. The contrast between these two signs is strong, but each of them has an important part to play. The Virgos are the natural healers of the zodiac; their ability to take care of the sick and understand the practical aspects that need to be dealt with in life is immense. 2012–2020 is a marked period of readjustment for us all, and a healing process needs to take place within all of our internal worlds before our external is healed and experienced as different. The outward abilities of Virgo are important as well as their own survival techniques, because without the Virgo's input we are left with a chasm of practical application. Virgo is ruled by the planet Mercury – the 'winged messenger of the gods' – who delegates and enables communication between humans. In a way Virgo is in that mould, but different from its cousin Gemini, who is also ruled by Mercury. The difference is temperament: Gemini is an air element and the Virgo is the earth. This means that the Virgo grasps ideas by approaching them with a stern practicality; for instance, can they be used for everyday use? To what extent can an idea help humanity develop? This is the great skill of the Virgo, because they are realists in the nicest way. However, there is one planet that could scupper this ability and cause misdirection for the Virgo. The opposite sign of Virgo is Pisces and during the next eight years Neptune (the planet of illusions) is travelling through the sign of Pisces. Now depending on which date you were born during the Sun's cycle through the constellation of Virgo, the effect of

Neptune is quite opposite to that of the pragmatic Virgo. This puts a fuzzy logic on the Virgo's proceedings, so that this sign starts to realise the spiritual potential of Neptune. The Virgo's gift is being able to put abstract concepts into a practical form. However, the Neptune influence could see them rebelling against their natural thinking, causing a conflict with their inner resources that others around them may find hard to understand. Virgos understand on a deep level the hypothesis of service to others, but may get confused in their thinking and completely let go of preconceptions of the ego, thereby becoming a service for a higher purpose. This calls for a new thinking process as regards what it means to be under the rays of a Virgo. For no person is directly Virgo; it is rather the spiritual lessons that one must learn through the eyes and basic responses of the Sun sign, or more importantly the natal chart and the planets' aspects and transits. Through the energies and symbolism of a Sun sign we can begin to understand our development as a whole and to sense the direction of where humanity is going. The Virgo over the next eight years needs to shift its consciousness, in thought and action, and to realise new skills that are at his or her disposal. The Virgo being of earth nature likes to question everything and analyse every detail. If you ask a Virgo how they are feeling they will normally respond by saying, 'I don't know, let me think about it.' They question through the realm of logic rather than give a spontaneous emotional reaction. This is part of their personal make-up, and also their survival technique (which all signs have). But during 2012–2020 those natural reactions could change and a much more emotional response could spring from the mind of the Virgo. The Neptune cloud puts a twist on the Virgo making this sign much more responsive to higher vibrations and creative thinking. This could lead to an internal revolution within the Virgo, which as a symbolic figure could help to heal us all.

Libra

Libra is the sign of balance as depicted by the symbol of the scales; this reinforces the need to create harmony and diplomacy. Libra is also an air sign that needs to mentally communicate with others. The period 2012–2020 is a time when balance and diplomacy will be needed like no other time before. Libra is mentally bright and can see both sides of an argument, but can also 'sit on both sides of the fence'. Within the first half of 2012, Saturn can have a limiting energy around the Sun sign it is placed in, because is still travelling in the sign of Libra. It is only in October 2012 that we begin to see Saturn shift in to Scorpio, which will come as a blessing to most Librans. But this is just the start of their personal journey towards the crisis point. Librans are not very good at conflict on a personal or global level, yet they seem to be a sign that is always in the firing line of conflict between different personalities. It is as if they are destined to fight battles with others around them, and this seems to come as a great surprise to Librans. But the message is to rise above all that is happening and have a cool head with it. In July 2013 Jupiter enters Cancer which will naturally form a square aspect to the Libran's Sun. This will cause a tense period of over-expanding oneself to feed the ego's need for self-gratification, and although not totally negative this can lead to a certain reliance on luck. The air signs (Gemini, Libra and Aquarius) always have the ability to stand apart from the chaos as if they are the audience in life's trials and tribulations. This is a gift and in some ways an Achilles heel of which they need to be aware. Unlike the Aquarian, the Libran needs people around them and it is through this impetus that the Librans over the next eight years will be able to excel. The Libran cycle is an important one where harvest time is celebrated and the days start to get colder. The Libran wants the warmth of summer and the cold of winter; this means they need people to communicate with but also an opportunity to step back from emotional situations in order to seek that mental balance. This is exactly the mantra that will be used by Librans to get the best results over the next eight years. In September 2016 and for the next year Jupiter will be passing through Libra which should help them to redefine who they are and expand their own consciousness. The other major theme for Librans is Uranus travelling in their opposite sign of Aries; this patrols the axis between how we view ourselves (ascendant) and how others view us (descendant). Uranus is not a planet that sleeps quietly, it is an electric shock that can jolt us into a new reality or overcharge our nervous system. The importance of this aspect is that Librans will expect to find that those around them are rebelling against their (the Librans) principles causing upset and strife; therefore a certain 'Zen' approach to those close to them is essential. Uranus is teaching Librans to be more spontaneous and decisive in their thoughts and actions, bringing about renewal in the way they deal with others and the way that they relate. This energy puts the emphasis on dealing with others people's ideas, emotions and in some ways insecurities. So we come back to the two words that are associated with Libra: diplomacy and balance. Over these next eight years do not let Uranus take you off balance.

Scorpio

It must be said that Scorpio is one sign that (normally) deals with transformation and change well, in fact it even revels in it. So you would think that Scorpio would find the 'crisis point' a breeze compared to the other signs. Scorpio is a fixed sign, so as long as the Scorpio is the one that is initiating the change then all is well and good. But if the change is coming from another person or a situation that the Scorpio does not have control over, then that becomes a problem. Scorpio needs to feel in tune with life at a deeper level than most because with the Scorpio there is always a lot going on beneath the surface. So the Scorpio becomes naturally intuitive and is able to pick up world events as well. So in these pressing times the Scorpio might feel that they are picking up everyone else's vibrations but their own. However, the Scorpio is a sign that can transform others' lives by being part of them – we could say everyone needs a least one Scorpio in their life. The next eight years will be a period of growth and change for all of us, as Pluto, Scorpio's natural ruler, is travelling through the sign of Capricorn. The relationship between Scorpio and Capricorn is one that is heavy but can also achieve great results. The reason for this is that both signs are hard workers that are ambitious in energy and status. Pluto wants to reveal the inner workings of whatever sign that it is passing through, and as discussed in earlier chapters, Capricorn is a sign that rules governmental institutions. Of all of the signs in the zodiac, Scorpio is the most likely to rebel against authority during this period in time. This is the reaction of Scorpio to the planet Pluto's (its ruler) journey through Capricorn, also, because of the water and earth elements that are combined here, some kind of growth will occur. The emotional element in 2012–2015 will be heightened due to the extreme behaviour of Pluto. This is also affected by Saturn travelling through Scorpio, so in astrological terms we have a mutual reception, meaning that two ruler planets are travelling through each others' signs. This accentuates the planets' energies that are involved, ie Saturn and Pluto. Scorpio will be very conscious of these motivations to destroy and rebuild all that is around them. The period between 2012 and 2015 will see violent demonstrations, extreme terrorism, and the death of governments. Also, more economic disasters, earthquakes will occur and various environmental issues will be highlighted. Pluto and Saturn in this period start to do battle from 2014–2015; the intense rays between these two are almost magnetic and yet are totally controlled by 'other' forces. This is symbolic of the need for power and an obsessive quality; this happens when these two planets are prominent. On an individual level, if you are born with the sign of Scorpio, to survive you must let go of the preconceptions of who you are and not get yourself into ego battles with other people, for it is only a projection that you are developing in a negative sense. Your inner insecurities could well be very much at the surface of your thinking instead of lurking beneath the radar. Learning to appreciate and even gain strength from this could help you to become more whole within your personality. The Scorpio, if it is to help others, must realise his/her own darker aspects within the soul, and then confront and transform them into a positive light. The Scorpio wants to merge with others because of its need to have a union with another or an ideal. This is a motivating factor in getting what they want from life. Therefore the next eight years could see the Scorpio rise from the mythological Phoenix ashes once more.

Sagittarius

The symbolism behind the Sagittarius is the archer who directs his or her ideas with a flurry of energy and inspiration. The need for Sagittarians to express themselves is strong, and is often expressed in colourful ways that give rise to optimism and insight. However, for many Sagittarians (those who have this sign strong in their charts) there may be a different or more restrained energy coming from the Jupiter-born. This to a certain degree is due to the influence of Saturn, the planet that can put a dampener on the Sagittarian party. But sometimes we need to focus on the more serious aspects of life. This is where the archer has much to learn during this period because at best the archer is the teacher of the zodiac, who has much knowledge to pass on to others. Sagittarius is a fire sign and mutable, therefore it is adaptable and is a natural leader especially in the fields of education, and metaphysical subject matters. During the years 2012–2015 Saturn is in their solar twelfth house; this is the house of self-undoing and is a house that is very much the ruler of more unconsciousness matters. Saturn wants the Sagittarius to be prepared to begin a new cycle, but before that can happen there needs to be a planetary agreement that states that the Sagittarian needs to be more open and less demanding on their personal identity. This is because the archer in basic terms is not to sure who he/she really is, especially if alone. The lesson is for them to be comfortable within their own internal structure; that is what Saturn is doing with their solar twelfth house. In 2015 Saturn enters your first house, the house that directs your energy level and in some ways your personality. Saturn brings structure to the proceedings or a least a psychological need to create structure for the archer in your life. This is an important evolution in the Sagittarian's cycle for it brings about a real sense of responsibility to their world view. The start of a new cycle begins that will last nearly thirty years for the Sagittarius. How you respond to this will determine the outcome and choices that you make to manifest your future. Jupiter is a planet that can bring that luck and goodwill to you as long as you do not abuse its power and indulge in it. But the main point is that Jupiter works best when it is working with Saturn, because the two energies can accomplish a great deal together, in fact you could say that they come as a package. Saturn in your first house creates stability in thought and action that leads to success after a two-and-a-halfyear mini-cycle. The archer needs to embrace these changes and help to bring moral and social structure to communities that they inhabit; it is an important contribution that they can make to the world's eight-year crisis points.

Once Saturn has passed through the first house in 2018 the archer can then begin to concentrate on its resources and its ability to consume and build its knowledge and ideas. This is the sign that will really make a difference over this period in how we live and what types of material we use. This is the sign of the eco-warriors.

Capricorn

How can one survive if the planet that rules the underworld is travelling through your own sign? That may be a question that Capricorns areasking themselves. Indeed we are all becoming aware of the importance of Pluto in Capricorn and how it has kick-started the disintegration and displacement of society and its rules, and shown us how authority can have too much power. The point is that as an astrological evolution we need to go through this cycle in order to survive; the world cannot continue down the road that it is going without some internal struggle and destruction taking place, it's almost a natural process. However, one aspect that could be conceived is that Capricorns if they are not careful could become too comfortable with Pluto's power and drive. This could lead to an unhealthy need to control, what I am trying to say is that Capricorns could feel like they are getting what they want. This could be due to the undercurrents (Pluto) and motivations of dominance that may takeing them to a darker place. How they deal with this increase in energy and the guiding need to exploit the weaknesses in others could become much more apparent. What I am saying is that Capricorns may not act on these impulses, but may pick up these energies from the collective unconsciousness. It is as if Capricorns are antennae for what the powers that be are thinking, therefore they will feel a heavy burden placed on them that detracts from what they really want. This will lead to many Capricorns dropping out of the 'system' over the course of the next eight years. This might seem to contradict many of the aspects of Capricorns' desires and drives, but the reason is that Pluto's passage through their own sign is essentially about personal as well as universal transformation. Therefore the reaction under the rays of Pluto could be extreme and revolutionary. Even in the last twenty years the sign Capricorn has had to shift priorities and goals to suit the ever-changing world, leading to a split in the descriptive elements and essence of the personality traits of this sign. One is the traditional, the 'worker' or the 'authoritarian' who seeks stability through action (cardinal) who has a drive for material success (earth). The other is more spiritual in his or her pursuit, preferring a minimal existence unfettered by the trivialities of mundane worries. This type of Capricorn wants to break free from Saturn's grip and limitations, while still climbing the proverbial mountain, in other wordswith a spiritual rather than a material aim. The basis for this change is true for all the signs of the zodiac, meaning world and planetary energies must change – nothing is static. So with this in mind the Capricorn will have to choose during this period which route it would like to take. In January 2018 Capricorn's ruler Saturn will enter its own sign meeting up with Pluto. This will be a testing time for all, as the heavyweights of the zodiac come together tough times will be had by all. However, with Capricorn you can expect a certain amount of reality checks, which can give us the foresight of what we need to prioritise and so help us to build our new future. The 'state' becomes under threat from the planetary energies that are intoxicated by the need for power and control, namely those of Saturn and Pluto. But if Capricorn builds these empires it is also Capricorn that can destroy the old and begin again with the help of Aquarius to bring in the new age.

Aquarius

There is a very direct relationship between the Capricorn and the Aquarius that creates a bridge of truth – let me explain. Capricorn is ruled by Saturn and in traditional astrology Saturn was also the planetary ruler of Aquarius. These two signs cover the period from late December to late February. This is a period of the cold winter frost, when the scarcity of the land brings a more frugal attitude to our lives. Therefore the relationship between the two is very close; the Capricorn understands the need to save for the future, but the Aquarius intuitively under-stands that spring is just round the corner, when new life takes shape and the land is more fruitful. In the last sentence we have a perfect description of the Aquarius, because this sign is the seer of the zodiac. Aquarians can foresee the future and place great faith in its ability to provide us humans with what we need. When all is lost the Aquarius has the faith for things to get better. There is a coolness around the Aquarius like with the Capricorn individual, but a certain amount of hidden knowledge is also present; these people have magnetic personalities and always come across as if they know something that you don't or are not even aware of. Aquarius understands the complexities of humankind but can also detach enough to help others through life. The skills thatAquarians have will be needed more after 2020 when the crisis point hits a high note and we as humans have to begin to believe that just round the corner are 'new fruits' growing for our needs. This is the energy that Aquarius is working through. Over the last thirteen years, Aquarians have made major shifts and had many tribulations due to the planets Uranus and Neptune passing through their own sign. However, both planets are now firmly placed in the signs of Aries and Pisces. This frees Aquarius up to start to emerge during this time with fresh radical ideas that can be important factors in how we develop. There have been many theories about when the Aquarian age started or when it is due to start. On a personal note regarding this debate, I believe that the start of the Aquarian age points to around 1904. Since that time we have see great advances in technology, and also two World Wars that have changed our world forever. We have seen a great cultural change, the defining moment of this is of course the 1960's with music, electrically inspired (Uranus). We must remember that Aquarius has two rulers, Saturn and Uranus, and both have an almost push and pull energy – one structure, the other revolution. Since 1904 in the western world we have seen a breakdown in religion, in particular Christianity, which was the totem of the age of Pisces. This has given rise to an interest in occult science and 'new age' techniques for the new millennium. Aquarius is a powerful sign that is an air element that increases communications and is fixed in purpose, meaning that it is able to gain results through determined action. However, the Aquarius' energy can also be quite perverse; it likes to challenge authority, in many ways it is the internal struggle of Uranus trying to change Saturn that fuels Aquarius, but this can lead to fanatical behaviour in the name of truth. The seer becomes the sinner, who explodes into action just for the sake of 'something', no matter what it is changing. When we think of Uranus it is like having electricity running through our veins. Anybody who was born with this sign dominating their natal chart will feel that they are about to overcharge on these electric currents and that an outlet is needed. Aquarians' role over the next eight years is to believe and remain optimistic about the future, and it is also to point us in the right direction based on idealistic principles. For after 2020 the Aquarian nature will be desperately needed.

Pisces

When everything gets too tough you always have Neptune to comfort and help you escape from the tyranny of Pluto. We now come to the sign when the night force of life is at its darkest, when the metaphorical owls come out and oversee the state we are in before disappearing into the night. The Pisces has an important role, but the question remains: does Pisces want to pursue that role or would they rather swim away? The emblem is Neptune, their planetary ruler, which is placed in their own sign over this eight-year cycle. The word 'transcend' is a word that encapsulates the sign of Pisces; its meaning is to 'go beyond' and this is how the Pisces tackles life, with less boundaries than us mere mortal eleven previous zodiac signs. However, there are important lessons and survival techniques that need to be implemented in order for us to gain from 2012–2020 and beyond. In all honesty if you are a Pisces and are reading this section only, I suggest you read the previous sign of Aquarius to gain a more rounded understanding of your placement in the zodiac. For you will see that we have the optimism of Aquarius that develops as the Sun passes to the sign of Pisces, whereby the impetus is a sort of melting from the form of what it means to be human, at least that is the 'want'; the reality is that Pisces is a mixture of all of the zodiac signs. That is why when you meet a Pisces they can be as direct as an Aries, as philosophical as a Sagittarius, as changeable as a Gemini, self-indulgent like a Taurus, or as critical as a Virgo. This is an aspect of the Pisces make-up that they need to understand, ie the Pisces identity soaks up the reactions of 'others', allowing the Pisces to mimic personality traits found in people with whom they interact and communicate. With this in mind the Pisceans can find it difficult to get to grips with their identity, they have difficulty knowing who they really are. Neptune will become an infusion of the deeply spiritual and the indecisive, but realising which of Neptune's rays you are under will help you to carve out your role in this world crisis point. The point of the rather obvious role of Neptune passing through Pisces is of course the end of the cycle before we enter a more Arian period. Pisces need to embrace their contribution. It is subtle and passive but quite formidable, for without faith we are swimming in a sea without a lifeboat. Pisces are able to bring that comfort and longing for a union with a God form that unites us all through redemption and leads us to paradise. It is my own assumption that the astral world is closely connected to Neptune and Pisces, because it is a reality that is created by the higher self depending on the energies that have been absorbed in a lifetime. The astral world is a place that creates richness in colour, vibration and form that transcends the ordinary. The journey to the astral world is usually taken at night time when the person is asleep (twelfth house Pisces) although it can be participated in or induced in a waking state through magical practice. But upon entering the astral realm we must 'trust' in the process of the higher self before we can enter it. During this dalliance with trust we experience elementals that can cause upset and drain energy from the higher self. The dangers are there but it is how we respond to them that counts, and usually they take the form of our being controlled and dominant in what we do want and what we do not wish for. Once we have overcome our initial trust issues we can begin to enter the astral world and experience a new reality and an explosion of our senses. Once in the astral world it is hard to think of wanting to go back to our heavy shell-like physical body because in the astral realm we feel light, free and unrestricted; we also hear musical sounds that cannot be comprehended in the physical world. We of course have entered into a higher dimension that can be accessed at any time and at any point through meditation and visualisation. Within the astral world (from personal experience) we experience emotions of joy to fear and more; we can access points in time in the past, present or future, for the boundaries are no longer available, we are the creator of them. The astral world is heavy in Neptunian conception, the vibration of its rays and its own Moons helps to create the astral world, because that is the world which is the next entrance for humans once our cycle is ended on Earth. The moons Triton and Nereid have a cosmic effect on the astral rays; this is based on the watery element of Neptune and Pisces that signals the emotional pull of the astral world, for the emotions still live on but the physical body is of no use. We experience a sense of liberation that upon being in this realm can influence our vision of the physical world (if we come back to the physical realm). The point is that those under the sign of Pisces, or those with a heavy Neptune in their charts, are attuned to the astral world and at points in their life wish to escape. This is because they understand that as humans our next development (evolution) is to enter the astral world. Pisces recognises this but is also aware that not everyone is ready for that leap. Pisces need to be the gatekeepers to the next dimension and that is why psychics, clairvoyants, mediums and Tarot readers are born with strong Pisces/Neptune themes in their charts; they are the gatekeepers who have been to the new dimensions and can assist others through that journey. There is a massive chasm between the planets Mars at the beginning of the zodiac cycle and Neptune at the end. But as the Tree of life suggests the Mars energy is directed by Malkuth and Neptune by Kether the supreme one. Our need to enter into the 'other' realm is guided by music, poetry and spiritual practices, but Pisces is there to remind us that it is all around us and quite easy to access once the trust issue has been dealt with. This is where the astrological dynamics of the universe speak for themselves; the universe is infinite and encompasses a whole host of different dimensions that the higher self can enter into. Neptune's passage through Pisces will help to create that bridge and access, for those wishing to go beyond. There are of course dangers within this, one being the pitfall of not being grounded or ready to deal with the physical reality of life once we have experienced the astral world. This is a permanent feature in Pisces' psychological state; even if they are not consciousness of it. For the Pisces as a symbol and as an individual has experienced and entered the astral world and is restless to go back there, forming a faith that is unbreakable and giving them the ability to sacrifice, because they know that there is more to this life.

The emergence of Uranus in Aries, Neptune in Pisces and Pluto in Capricorn will increase and engage a wider audience in more consciousness thinking and more individuals being able to connect to higher realms and higher beings. This leads to a greater acceptance of what we now call 'new age philosophies', but without the commercial drive. The new age market is now an industry that will have to make a major shift. It boomed in the early to mid-nineties when Uranus and Neptune were in Capricorn, and now Pluto is going to have to tear down those structures. That will leave us all in a state of flux in the West as we must now search more internally instead of externally; but the old masters return to give us lost knowledge. This takes us back to another Neptunian myth and that is the previous incarnation of the lost city of Atlantis, sunk by the wrath of the sea god Poseidon. These are lessons that we must now learn as we are already sinking, metaphorically speaking, into our own capitalist bubble. Neptune in Pisces seeks to distil and if not heard will create waves for us all, emotional or environmental. Uranus is seeking new life in Aries; its lightning bolts are hoping to install courage and a willingness to move forward with an electrifying pace. The dynamics of the universe are changing and the sign Aries is at the forefront of this major shift. As I said before, Aries is at the beginning of a new cycle, Pisces is at the end, but because the wheel of the zodiac is a circumference we have two points, the beginning and the end, which meet to create an energetic shift and directness in rays. The symbolism is of death and rebirth; this is seen through nature and its cycles but also through the planets' journeys. This begs the question without even including the planet Pluto: are we indeed at a period in time of new starts and old endings? Pluto is quite literally the earth that is holding us all together, trying to embrace the traditional structures. We have conquered science and the tangible, now we come to a time when we must explore within the mainstream of society the non-rational. The dance that we are now experiencing is a dance that will take the mind to many places, where the emotions will soar and the spirit will be set free. The cycle of the zodiac indicates how this is depicted and instigated and to what purposes for our collective consciousness.

The extremity of the years 2012–2020 I have aptly named the crisis point, fearing that the importance of this time would be lost in the translation of astrological symbolism. However, it is also a need to fully comprehend the timing of events and the significance of this period in such a way that can have a bearing on how we all live our lives. Throughout this time many positive events and movements will help us to overcome these planetary energies and give us understanding that will help future generations. One of the major factors is how as humans we are able to balance these different and contrasting rays so that we may find peace of mind and inner security. I believe that 'The Solar Way' is to be installed, but different from the more eastern philosophies and Buddhist thinking. The Solar Way is working with the dynamic energies of the planets through the higher self and the chakra system by bringing these energies to our earthly plane, ie not trying to escape from the physical to the other realms but bringing them into practical form. The ethos behind this is that by allowing and digesting these rays we are using them to help us come to a greater understanding spiritually while remaining committed to our physical obligations and commitments. This allows a freedom in thought and action through simple exercises that can help us to follow the path of the Solar Way. This path does not consist of escaping from our environment but rather will release us from the anxiety of the ebb and flow of these energy shifts. The Solar Way is created as a survival guide for the new cycle that we are experiencing.

The point of the Solar Way is using the power of the planets to energise and assist us, as the planets are living bodies full of energy. To harness their rays it is a process of understanding how they operate and how they can help you. The first steps are through an intuitive understanding of the meanings of each planet and how each planet affects our daily rhythms and lives. The combatative element of the astrological energies is forcing us as humans to look further into ourselves in dealing with our perceptions of the world. Becoming a vessel for the planets' rays can assist in realising the true force of their effect on our everyday lives. Being centred is allowing the energies of the Solar System to flow through our consciousness. For example certain planets rule certain days of the week and this can give us a real insight in planning events for a particular day.

Monday – Moon
Tuesday – Mars
Wednesday – Mercury
Thursday – Jupiter
Friday – Venus
Saturday – Saturn
Sunday – Sun

The above table is an indicator of which planets rule a certain day (you can also break this down to the hours in the day). So if you were to book an interview, then the planet of communication, Mercury, rules the day of the week Wednesday, meaning that a good period to use the fullness of Mercury's vibration for your interview would be on Wednesday. Venus is good for love matters and also social activities, and Saturn is very good at getting things done and achieving aims. It is therefore a pity that we do not (generally speaking) have Saturday as a work day in the western world. We would do better to swap it with Monday which is ruled by the fluctuating nature of the Moon that on this day really wants to deal with domestic matters.

Knowing how the planets affect our day to day lives can have a major impact on how we deal with life's tribulations. The Solar Way allows the participant to acknowledge and understand these vibrations and can therefore make life's cycles easier to cope with. Within this book the outer planets of Uranus, Neptune and Pluto have been marked out as energies that are pushing humanity into a number of different directions that challenge our needs and our morals. The Solar Way puts less emphasis on an individual way, but concentrates on a collective energy that can be directed by the masses, not by a small group or elite. Getting in touch with the planets in symbolic terms can help you to understand how they can help you, this means taking time to get used to the rhythm of each planet. Over the next eight years humanity is going to go through a major shift and transformation, with a breakdown of conventional religion and a distrustfulness of governmental bodies. This will cause initial confusion and panic in many, leading to a breakdown in fundamental principles. The need to understand cycles within an astrological context (as in the past) will lead to a much more realistic path, one that is free from imposed restrictions. However, first we must face the fears and limitations before the full practice of the Solar Way and its understanding of the cosmos and how we as humans respond to it becomes common.

Chapter 12

'The Stars that Play with Laughing Sam's Dice'
Jimi Hendrix, 1967

There is the psychological stage in life that has been coined the 'dark night of the soul' which describes a state when one realises one's deepest fears and anxieties. Another way of understanding this process from an astrological viewpoint is when Pluto comes knocking on our front door and hands us a final demand in life. During the period 2012–2020 great adjustments will need to be made in relation to how we view our futures on this planet Earth. The cardinal quality that we are experiencing (Uranus in Aries, Pluto in Capricorn and at the time of writing Saturn in Libra) is causing major shifts but also destructive tendencies. Our metaphorical dice has thrown too many 'ones', leading to a tardiness in moving forward, ie our own development is lagging behind. Pluto, Uranus and Saturn are playing with our deepest fears about where we fit in within our internal and external structures. One cycle begins (Uranus in Aries) and yet one ends (Neptune in Pisces), but the question is: how will this change our views and behaviour?

Neptune in Pisces will bring about a new form of 'new age' thinking, and this will be emphasised over the next fourteen years within the framework of other dimensions being discovered and acknowledged by scientists. The need to become more engaged in higher states of consciousness and astral travel will filter down in society as something that can be experienced by everyone. Neptune will dissolve the boundaries that were previously in place. In 1848 Spiritualism became wildly popular and opened up a whole host of different interests, including mediumship, clairvoyance, paranormal research and ghost hunts; there were also numerous fraudsters. The masculine principle of Uranus in Aries will help to redefine the gender of the masculine, therefore brining in much more equality in the western world. But Uranus rebels against the system and will do anything to be heard and to express its energy.

The years 2012–2017 will mark the height of the crisis point; this is when the governmental bodies will have to justify many of their actions from the past. This will be because what the public was informed of in the past by the institutions will have to be scrutinised, because of certain trials. The United States of America in 2016 will go through a crisis in leadership and with their allies, causing concern and frustration in the American people. In December 2017 Saturn will enter Capricorn allowing the shift of energy within the world to concentrate on traditional values; structure will become a mantra, like the Conservative's phrase 'back to basics' in the early nineties. The struggle to employ old structures will cause the public to question every policy that is implemented. Public-run services in Britain will be severely tested to the limit as the business world dominates most of our living, from education and health to the prison service, in the period 2013–2018. By 2014 a new political party that uses socialist principles (Uranus in Aries) will come into force, with a leader who is younger in appearance that his years. This party in Britain will cause havoc for other political parties because they will tear down the old structures and unveil secrets of the old views on how to run a political party. We will see the early beginnings of a new way of running western countries. Environmental policies will be pushed through in Europe and the States creating wealth and employment from 2016 onwards. Solar-powered devices will change the way that we each live and engage with our immediate environment. Transport will be revolutionised, becoming cheaper and easier to run from 2018 and beyond, starting off in northern Europe before moving to England and the States. The health sector comes to a crisis point of its own in the States as well as in this country, with regulations replacing moral judgements, leading to decisions being made in terms of finance and investment. The hub of this will be a need to re-educate the way that we heal the body through the mind and the emotions. Waiting lists will go up and the elderly in society will be given more control over their life-span leading again to moral obligations and a re-evaluation of how society can be reconstructed. During this time the general public becomes weary with excuses and starts to take matters into their own hands. Technology starts to use the concept of living a separate life (Neptune) through the advancement of virtual worlds leading to a younger generation who are more concerned with their inner virtual world rather than the real world and society as a whole. The Neptune rays passing through Pisces allow escapist tendencies, because the outer world is constrained with regulations and rules. These are the negative aspects of Neptune in Pisces, but if they are used as a positive influence then we can reach new heights in terms of spirituality and sacrifice in the name of a higher cause. These are the two sides of the coin that Neptune can throw at us, and depending on which energy each of us veers towards we will see the eventual outcome for the future. The planet Pluto is the dominating factor in the heavens, causing friction and turmoil in our lives because of its passage through the zodiac sign of Capricorn. When you dance with Pluto you had better be careful of the flames, because the symbolism behind the planet is one of rejuvenation through self-examination. The speed of western culture will begin to make people feel dizzy within their own equilibrium, as the first three chakras of the Base, Sacral and Solar Plexus dominate our consciousness. After the period of 2020 on a collective basis we move up to the heart chakra that links with the throat chakra creating a better understanding of our human and spiritual needs. This is also directed by Neptune's vibrations, but we must remember that Neptune will find it difficult with the dominance of Uranus and Pluto; this will create periods of 'snippets' of Neptune's energy.

The world during these transits might feel like a massive adjustment is taking place, or a feeling of healing through destruction. The planet Uranus travels in Aries, starting a new cycle which brings about and creates a new way of experiencing planet Earth and beyond. In the last forty years we have seen many upheavals and technological advancements already, as the planets react to how we as humans respond to their energies. If we as a race choose to act in a negative way to these vibrations, then this will cause a repetitive cycle of chaotic thinking and reacting. However, if we choose to allow the natural flow of transformation to take place, this can lead to a new dawn in the state of our world view, that allows humans to evolve and develop in a spiritual sense. For this to take place the emergence through Neptune of Pisces' rays – a new understanding of the cosmos and the unseen in the world – needs to bear fruition. At times during these next eight years it may feel that we are being bombarded with a constant flurry of anxiety and deception. But these 'feelings' and gut reactions allow us to tap into a higher source that leads to a greater understanding of the less tangible aspects of life and the universe. The revelation that there is more to life than meets the eye starts to resonate and to be questioned by more individuals, helping to raise the consciousness. The planets are merely the portals that help us to understand ourselves and the world that we exist in.

2020 will mark a time when everyone will have a better perspective on life's trials and tribulations but will also be a period when governmental bodies need to adjust their principles to fit in with the new way of existing. Even after 2020 we will still have lots of work to do; the planets are still moving in the Solar System and therefore will still have a profound affect on our lives as a whole and as individuals. But it will be the case that the rebuilding of society will start to take place slowly, for there will still be unrest and revolutions. But only in reaction to what has happened in the past, indeed our basic needs will need to be met as humans, and it is with this requirement that the 'shift' in our lives will bring about a world that will evolve, leading to our external view of the world becoming bigger through our spiritual experiences.

Chapter 13

Aftermath

After periods of change and transformation there is only one way that the world that we all inhabit can go. Through many centuries and many 'crisis points' within our historical lineage we have evolved, developed and tried to learn. Some lessons are harder than others, and as a collective we must all strive to live with generosity, acceptance and love. The planets' rays enable us to have a direct link with higher sources and energies that ultimately can help us to begin the process of spirituality, as we become more awakened to our inner selves and of course our outer world.

After the year 2020 there will be a need to start to rebuild the fundamental structures of how we live, as well as to focus on our expectations and perceptions. The process of restructuring will take time, but then our hard work will start to take form and help to shape our existence. Pluto's journey through Capricorn will be at 23 degrees by December 2020. The orbit of Pluto will be at the latter degrees of Capricorn, meaning that we are sub-ruled by Mercury's vibrations which help to negotiate communication between adverseries. Once Pluto accesses Aquarius in 2023 a more humanitarian concern will be the mantra of the world, for Aquarius is a fixed sign and Pluto rules the fixed sign of Scorpio, and this brings about change from determined efforts and perseverance. The energetic pull of this combination brings about results and a focus towards brotherhood within the structures of society.

But until that time we must all trust in the changes that we are about to experience, for the universe does not have one director but believes in the concept of union. Astrology embraces that, so why can't we?

Demian Allan
2012

Bibliography

Arroyo, Stephen, Astrology, Karma and Transformation, CRCS Publications 1978

Baigent, M, Campion, N, Harvey, C, Mundane Astrology, Thornsons, 1984

Lofthus, M, A spiritual Approach to Astrology, CRCS, 1983

Michelsen, Neil, The American Ephemeris for the 2oth Century , ACS Publications, 1983

Michelsen, N, The New American Ephemeris 2007 -2020, Starcrafts Publishing, 2007

Orr, Majorie, The Astrological History of the World, Vega, 2002

Rudhyar, Dane, The Pulse of Life, Servire, 1963

Rudhyar, Dane, New mansions For New Men, First House Edition, 1978

References

UK's Chart - The United Kingdom, 00.00 LT, 1 January 1801, Westminster, 51N30, 0W07. The coming into force of the Union of Great Britain and Ireland.

US' Chart – United States of America, 17.10 LMT, 4 July 1776, Philadelphia, 39N57, 75W10.

Mundane Astrology, Baigent, Campion, Harvey, Thorsons, 1984.

Thank you to Astrolabe for your kind permission of software for charts.

BOOKS

O is a symbol of the world, of oneness and unity. In different cultures it also means the "eye," symbolizing knowledge and insight. We aim to publish books that are accessible, constructive and that challenge accepted opinion, both that of academia and the "moral majority."

Our books are available in all good English language bookstores worldwide. If you don't see the book on the shelves ask the bookstore to order it for you, quoting the ISBN number and title. Alternatively you can order online (all major online retail sites carry our titles) or contact the distributor in the relevant country, listed on the copyright page.

See our website **www.o-books.net** for a full list of over 500 titles, growing by 100 a year.

And tune in to myspiritradio.com for our book review radio show, hosted by June-Elleni Laine, where you can listen to the authors discussing their books.

MySpiritRadio